9 Creativity-Required Businesses You Can Start From Home

and How to Make Them Profitable Careers

By Bill Watson

First Edition

**Creative Books, P.O. Box 463 Beaver, Pennsylvania
15009-0463**

9 Creativity-Required Businesses You Can Start From Home

and How to Make Them Profitable Careers

By Bill Watson

Published by:

▼ Creative Books
P .O. Box 463
Beaver, PA 15009-0463

Copyright © 1999 by Willam E. Watson
Library of Congress Catalog Number: 99-94895
Photography: Rhonda Watson
Publisher's Cataloging in Publication Data
Watson, William E.
9 Creativity-Required Businesses You Can Start from Home: and How to Make Them Profitable Careers.-1st edition.
Includes Index
ISBN 0-9670751-6-5
1. New Business Enterprises-Handbooks, Manuals, etc. 1. Title
1999
First printing: August 1999
Second printing: April 2001

Printed in the USA by

MORRIS PUBLISHING

3212 East Highway 30 • Kearney, NE 68847 • 1-800-650-7888

Disclaimer

This book presents an overview of the subjects covered. Many people make a full-time living from each of the businesses reported on within these pages; however, there is no guarantee by the author or the publisher that *you* will be successful should you decide to pursue one of these opportunities. There are too many variables such as your level of enthusiasm, commitment, ability to persevere, changing business climates and other factors for the author or the publisher to make any guarantee about how your attempt to launch your business will turn out.

Every effort has been made to present the material as honestly and accurately as possible, but neither the author nor the publisher is responsible for any mistakes within the text.

The intention of this book is to provide a preview of each business detailed, not a complete guide. Should you decide to pursue one of these businesses, you must read more in-depth on that particular endeavor, read business management books, study tax laws that may apply to your business and research other pertinent general business information.

You will receive the most value from this book by reading it cover-to-cover. There is a great deal of general information that applies to any creative business in each chapter.

About The Author

Bill Watson has extensive experience working in creativity-required businesses. He started playing the guitar at age 12; wrote his first of several hundred songs at age 14; and was performing full-time by age 20. His song material has been accepted by publishers such as Atlanta-based Hit One Music (BMI) and recorded by various artists such as the new-country group, Sidewinder. His production company, Play It Again Demos, is one of the best demo studios in the business and has completed song productions for thousands of satisfied clients.

In 1988 he founded a landscape nursery and lawn maintenance business which is still in operation.

During a five year stint self-publishing the <u>Listen Again Music Newsletter</u> and owning and operating the BMI song publishing company Listen Again Music, he began (and continues) writing articles, building credits that include the very biggest national magazines such as <u>Sports Afield</u>, <u>Income Opportunities</u>, <u>Entertainment News</u>, <u>Small Business Opportunities</u>, and many others.

Bill is currently fully self-employed and makes "a thoroughly enjoyable living" deriving all of his income from a combination of activities written about in this book.

Table of Contents

**Comments or questions can be sent to the author via e-mail:
bwats@forcomm.net**

Foreword

by Michael O'Connor

Most people who start businesses that have creativity as the core engine driving their income have no concrete idea of how to assess success. If you wanted to be an expert marksman, but could never hit the target, you'd probably realize that just maybe, being a sharpshooter wasn't for you. But, that's easy to figure out. Creativity-required endeavors don't have such an easily identifiable goal to aim for. As a prospective entrepreneur you may have nothing but a vague image of what "success" is, and only dreams to guide you.

The problem with dreams is that contrary to most beginner's beliefs, dreams alone won't be enough to sustain a career. Belief *is* the enthusiasm that keeps the creative fires burning, but you have to be aware that the creative arts are like an inverted pyramid with millions of people at the bottom. At each successive level, the attrition rate becomes enormous. Ultimately, your belief in your talents has to be wrapped in the cloak of some positive reaction from the leaders in whatever business you're trying to infiltrate.

In regards to the music business, most people (including myself when I started out), think that just getting the song to the secretary at a major label means we're inches away from a hit record. The only benefit of such ridiculous blind faith is that if we do not know we can't accomplish something, we come up with ways around the obstacles. But, that only happens in extremely rare cases. And we *all* think we're the rare case. For many years, before I really knew what was going on, I remember being very upset with the fact that someone wasn't knocking on my door saying, "By the way, we heard about how brilliant you are, here's a million dollars to share your genius with us." Ten years later when Berry Gordy offered me the dream of a lifetime, I turned him down. Go figure. It wasn't so much about being set for life and having money, it was not wanting to have my dreams blinded by the pot of gold waiting for me at the end of the rainbow. The fact that I had arrived and could finally claim that pot of gold, was beside the point. I thought...wait, I want to struggle some more, I can't sell out now, that would mean the journey's over and I've reached the peak of my travel.

What's weird is that these days the thrill of my getting to hear a record being produced by a famous producer is no more exciting than when in the early days of my struggle I was able to just place one of my songs in the hands of someone famous (even though I didn't know if they'd even like the song). Just getting to them was pretty exciting. Dreams are like a drug. The high starts to wear off unless the dosage keeps increasing. By dosage I mean an important event that transpires in your career to create excitement. In other words: 15 years ago it was a major thrill just to have a producer call me and tell me he liked my song. Now I only get that thrill when the producer has recorded the song and I know it's coming out as a single, then upon hearing it I feel it's a smash. We all need a bigger fix the longer we stay in the game. If I had ever gone longer than 2 years without progressing at least to the next level, I would have probably gotten out. Here was the time line for my level of thrills and successes:

1st year- Just to get my songs to the right people was a major high.

2nd year- To keep the same high I needed to hear producers say they were holding on to the song in hopes of recording it.

3rd year- At this point they had to say they were recording it, not just holding it.

4th year- Now they had to say not only were they recording it but that it was making the record.

5th year- Now they had to say that not only was the song making the record, but that it would be a single.

6th year- Now the single not only had to come out, but it had to hit the charts.

7th year- Now I was only happy when the song became a hit.

I'm numb to anything positive about my songs and/or music career unless I'm looking at the top 10 and see my song there. Otherwise, everything in my life is just ho, hum. Now my only problem is, that I will only be really happy if I have a hit on an artist that I release on my own record label. No matter what mountain peak you climb, you never really arrive. Why? Because your head clears the clouds and what do you see? Another mountain peak. The climb continues.

In my last year of college at UCLA, I was like millions of songwriters who felt that the songs I had written were hits and that I would see almost instant success. It was the same feeling you get when you buy a lottery ticket and you believe your number is destined to hit. In fact, I was clever enough to get into offices with a few industry heavyweights, but they were 100% unimpressed. Even though I was the one getting rejected, I believed *they* were the idiots, not me. With what I know now, if I had met with a guy like me, I would have thrown him out of my office. Here's a brief history of my inverted pyramid that started out as a guy with very little talent and a lot of belief:

After my last year at UCLA I moved in with Rick Nelson and his family and immediately started a career in the music business by opening the thousands of packages he had received from songwriters all over the country and started looking for songs for him. I didn't find one song in those thousands of packages from neophyte songwriters who had sent them to Rick in hopes of him finding a hit. I then went to all of the music publishers in town (who paid songwriters to write for them) and found a much higher caliber of song, but because Rick wasn't a big star anymore, the publishers were holding their best songs back for the big stars at the time. Because I was in their office they let me hear what a Barbara Streisand was holding, or a Karen Carpenter was going to be cutting. I heard such great songs. It was like a young tennis player watching aces being served. Because of that opportunity, I was able to pick up the artform.

I then went on the represent Glen Campbell's publishing company where I listened to another thousand songs from top publishers in the business and really got a sense of what the best writers in the business were writing. I then found my own writer, Leslie Pearl, who I felt was just as good as the best writers I had been hearing at the publishing houses. I put her on salary and we went to work developing a catalog of songs. Over the next two years she developed about 15 tunes for me- and I couldn't get a single recording. I got a few nibbles, but nothing started happening until the owner of a recording studio gave me free studio time allowing me to upgrade the quality of our demos.

After recording about 10 top-notch demos over the next two years, I began getting holds but no recordings. Six months later I was getting recordings, but no releases. Then with my first break- a Johnny Mathis record, I started to hit pay dirt. The songs I was developing with Leslie had reached about 40 songs, giving my catalog some depth. I started pitching my songs to all of the producers in town and calls started coming in from producers like Phil Ramone (Billy Joel, Barbara Striesand, Paul McCartney, Paul Simon) who told me he had a little movie that was perfect for one of my songs. The movie was *Flashdance*.

He cut the song *Manhunt* which won the writers a Grammy award and earned them each $250,000. Phil then recorded a song with Karen Carpenter that didn't get released for 15 years. When it did come out I sold it to BMG publishing for $15,000. Not only was I getting recordings with people like Kenny Rogers, Quincy Jones, Dr. Hook and the TV show Miami Vice, but my writer Leslie Pearl, was getting record offers (She went on to have a top 40 hit with the song "IF THE LOVE FITS" on RCA records). I then had a hit with Crystal Gayle entitled, "YOU NEVER GAVE UP ON ME"; a hit with Dr. Hook called "GIRLS CAN GET IT'" and signed artists to Polygram and Atlantic records. Berry Gordy, the founder of Motown started purchasing the publishing on a few of my songs at $10,000 a pop and then wound up offering me $500,000 for my entire catalog and the opportunity to start my own division at Motown (wanting to stay independent I turned him down). In the last three years I've been a staff writer/co-publisher for MCA (signed to the deal by Rod Stewart's management company) and have done publishing deals with BMG, where one of my published songs just got licensed to be on the television show Dawson Creek. And currently I have 3 songs on a new artist on Virgin Records being produced by world renowned producer David Kershenbaum (Tracy Chapman, Bryan Adams, Joe Jackson, Duran Duran).

Now to go from a dreamer with no ability to assess my own talents, to the credits I've just mentioned was not only because of my innate talent, but also my determination to stick with this business at the beginning when it didn't look very promising. Another huge factor: I was able to work out of my home. Working from home gave me low overhead, the ability to stay independent and other advantages home-based businesses enjoy that Bill discussed later in his book. In fact, I had my first hit record before I ever printed up any business cards and/or stationery. Why? With low overhead I was able to stay in business long enough to have a couple of recording artists- Rick Nelson and Glen Campbell- as my calling cards. Those names got me into the offices of people who would never have met with me otherwise. Once I learned from industry pros what I felt were the secrets of a hit record, I then attracted some of the biggest industry executives to contact me because they recognized my talent when they heard my songs. So it's not always what people can do for you, it's what you can learn from them that is the most valuable lesson to be learned.

My advice? Network with someone at the top of whatever profession you enter (and I mean do whatever it takes: errands, babysitting their kids, helping them with charity events, etc.) so that you have a reason to be around them, learn from them and co-opt their contacts. It's not easy...people in my position only have time to meet with new writers and/or artists who have been referred to us by people we respect and usually have known for the last 10 years. Here's the theory: if somebody can really do something for you, they're probably too busy to meet with you. But it can be done if you approach the person from the right angle rather than directly.

To sum it all up, it's the climbing of the mountain, not the arriving at the top, that's the real joy in life. There's a fire burning in you right now that can either produce nothing beyond the lumps of coal you fired it with, or that can produce diamonds if you stoke your fire with ample amounts of knowledge, action, creativity and perseverance. You will almost surely struggle at first but the rewards can be immeasurable. My advice? Go ahead, fire up that furnace.

Michael O'Connor is the owner of Michael O'Connor Music, P.O. Box 1869, Studio City, CA 91604. His book "The Michael O'Connor Newsletters" (How I Went from Rick Nelson's Barn to Barry Gordy's Mansion) with excellent inside information on the songwriting and publishing business is available through his company for $14.99 which includes postage and handling.

Introduction

One day I sat down at the computer and 9 months later a book with a strange title popped out. Of course, my first thought upon seeing what I'd created was, "Boy I'm lucky I didn't sit down at an incubator or something." But it also started me thinking... "What drove me to write this book?" Memories of scenes from years prior soon flooded my mind. I recalled many people asking many questions. I soon realized *exactly* what drove me to write this book.

This book was written to benefit two types of people: the person who is seeking a more fulfilling way to make a living, and the person who knows what they'd like to be doing but is clueless about how to go about it. And I'm assuming both types wish to start on a "shoestring" if possible.

It's written for the salesman who came nightly to hear a road band I was in at the Holiday Inn in Fort Wayne, Indiana. Obviously unhappy with his high-paying job, he grilled me practically every break to find out how he could go about learning to play. He wanted to join a road band.

It's written for the housewife from Georgia who once interrogated me about writing, wondering how she could get a start in the business.

It's written for teens in California who are trying to decide what to do with the first part of their life and it's written for the middle-age man in Michigan trying to decide what to do with the rest of his.

You are probably wrestling with the same types of thoughts. The desire to improve is a trait common to almost every person on this planet. It's only natural to ask questions that will help achieve that goal.

This book is my answer.

CHAPTER ONE

Why Should You Start A Creativity-Required Home Business?

On the surface the answer is a no-brainer: to make money, right? Well, it's not that simple. You could make money a lot of ways. And a lot faster. Let's get this fact out in the open right now- if you need money fast, a creativity-required business, or any business, is probably a bad choice.

Businesses take time to build. And they require an investment of both time and money long before they return profits to you. In spite of ads you may have seen in business opportunities magazines, businesses are rarely capable of making you rich quickly. If "getting rich quick" is what you're looking for, forget business and buy some lottery tickets. Just maybe you'll get lucky. Businesses are hard work.

THE BENEFITS

So, if a business won't make you rich quickly, why start one? First of all, being self-employed in your own successful business or career can give you everything a good job can- a reasonable amount of job security and a good income- plus a lot of other benefits, both tangible and intangible. A business can give you control of your work and life far beyond what most jobs can; an income above that of the average worker; an ability to profit from others labor rather than your own and a huge sense of achievement and accomplishment when you see your business succeed.

But why a home-based business? Low start-up costs are the biggest factor. Not having to pay rent at first, while letting your personal phone line and other personal items do double duty during the start-up phase can save enough money to mean the difference between success or failure.

An incentive for some people is the ability to watch a child while working. For others it might be an illness or disability that makes it difficult to commute to a work location. Only you can decide if a home-based business is right for you.

Certainly, most of the businesses in this book can be run successfully outside the home. While it is highly recommended to start from home, it's not an absolute impossibility to open a regular business location. If you are thinking of bypassing the home start-up phase, then read each chapter paying special attention to how long it takes to start seeing cash flow. Some of these businesses are best started at home because of the time it takes to see a return on your investment. For example, if you are writing articles for pay-on-publication magazines, rather than pay-on-acceptance ones, it can take many months to see your first check.

Variety: The spice of life

There are many business opportunities available to prospective entrepreneurs. Why start a creativity-required one? The best answer is: because when you use your God-given creativity to earn your income, the word "work" becomes synonymous with the word "fun". Would you prefer spending the majority of your time left on earth doing something enjoyable or something you find boring?

You probably aren't the type of person who would be happy turning out widgets on an assembly line all day or you wouldn't be reading this book to begin with.

You are most likely a person who's most happy when they not only have a say in the hours they work, but also like work best when each piece of it is a little different than the last. You crave variety. When things are too easy or too repetitive you become bored. And you definitely get excited when a project challenges you. If these descriptions fit you, then keep reading- your life is about to change for the better.

CHAPTER TWO

Can You Make A Living In A Creative Business?

Maybe you have a head start on beginning a creativity-required business. Perhaps you have a "green thumb," or write, or play an instrument. In fact, let's give you the benefit of the doubt and say you're good at what you do. You know you're good because your friends and relatives have told you so. Well, you might indeed be a good photographer or whatever, and that is a plus for sure. But can your talent-level truly be considered professional? And once you find out what's involved in using your talent to make a living, would you even want to? This book will help you answer those questions.

TALENT IS A FACTOR BUT...

But let's say you *don't* have a head start. Maybe you bought this book because you're curious- you've thought about becoming a writer or photographer or growing plants and figured this book is your chance to explore a little deeper into thoughts that have bugged you for years: Is there a better, more rewarding way for you to make a living? Is it realistic for you to think about making a living from something that seems more like fun than work? And even if some people do make a living at it, how can you compete with the people in paragraph one- the people with a head start over you?

You can take heart- and those of you with the head start can prepare for a dose of reality. First of all talent, no matter how awesome, is only one small part of the success equation. There are a lot of other factors that influence your ultimate success far more than talent does.

There are phenomenal songwriters who have never made dime one despite years of trying and there are mediocre songwriters who regularly cash hundred-thousand dollar royalty checks. There are great producers whose recording studios failed because they didn't know enough about business management and mediocre ones who are living in Beverly Hills. And there are world class guitarists working assembly lines and guitarists that barely know three chords playing concerts to full stadiums. Believe it. It's true.

What is it then if talent's not the deciding factor? Is it luck? No. Not hardly. Luck can sometimes play a part in how you get a break or two in your career but it's almost never the reason you end up *with* a career. The truth is- success is a combination of many things: The more talent you have, the better, but even more important factors like perseverance; knowledge of your field; knowledge of business in general and networking with others in your field usually determine your ultimate success. Those are the things that help you take advantage of the "lucky break" when it comes. And "lucky breaks" are usually the result of a good, consistent networking plan, rather than luck. Need proof? Read this report from a Pittsburgh paper:

* * *

November 30th, 1998, a Pittsburgh Pennsylvania guitarist, Cordell Dudley, died "without ever reaching the stardom he deserved" according to The Pittsburgh Post Gazette. Described as a "fiery, virtuosic guitarist" he rubbed shoulders with the likes of Jimi Hendrix' bassist, Billy Cox, in fact, Cox considered Cordell the best guitarist he'd jammed with since Hendrix.

Though everyone expected Cordell to break nationally, he came close several times but never quite got the break he needed. Norm Nardini, a Pittsburgh musician who did have a successful career had this to say of Cordell: "Just because you're a good musician doesn't mean you're a good businessman....As good a player as he was, he didn't have the business skills to keep himself in the better situations."

* * *

You will quickly find out that almost any creative endeavor is far more competitive than most other jobs or businesses. While you may be able to create something totally unique- a song, a photo, etc. you'll learn that there are few agents scouting for talent except scammers and rip-off artists. While your individual work may be unique, the fact you have talent isn't. Take the songwriting field for example. There are many thousands of people who are writing songs and actively submitting them to publishers at any given time. Yes, you can probably "make it" if you pursue songwriting, but if you have any illusions that it will be easy, you'd best rethink that position.

This book is written as if you will be working at the business you choose forty hours a week or more; however, you can start any of them part-time which is highly recommended. It will give

13

you a pressure-free opportunity to get to know what the business you choose is like before making the decision to go full time. If your talent isn't fully developed yet, starting at home in your spare time will give you time to develop your skills.

Marketing: the Achilles' heel of most creative people

To achieve success at any of the opportunities covered in this book, you will almost certainly have to master one skill above all others: marketing, which is *the* key to selling your product or service. Taking a fabulous photo or coming up with a great article idea *can* be a part of your marketing plan, but it's only a part. If you expect your work to sell itself simply because it's so great, your career will very likely resemble a pencil you accidentally sharpened into a three-inch stub- awfully short and certainly not worth the time you put into it.

CHAPTER THREE

Marketing- The Key To Success

Marketing is nothing but selling your work and making decisions that propel your career forward. It includes advertising but that's only part of it. It includes making a top-notch product or service but that is only part of it. The best way to define marketing is: marketing is everything you do in business that could possibly affect sales of your product or service.

MAYBE IT *IS* TIME TO GET THAT MUFFLER PUT BACK ON

Marketing could be the car you drive for business use. How? If you are a supposedly highly-successful artist giving a show and people are expecting to pay $50,000 for your paintings based on what they've heard about you, then they see you drive up in your '76 Chevy Nova, the one with the coat hanger holding the door on, well that just might *possibly* lead them to suspect that you aren't as successful as they had assumed. They

15

might decide not to buy a painting at any price. That's poor marketing. If you'd rented a new car for the show, your $50 investment would have preserved a $50,000 sale.

* * *

Marketing includes how you answer your phone. Let's say your potential prospect receives a sales pitch on letterhead that bespeaks of a large professional company whose products are quite expensive but well worth an investment in quality... *The* call comes in. Your 10-year-old answers the phone. The client asks to speak to you, and hears "Mommy's in the bathtub right now." In business, there's a phrase that perfectly describes the situation. It's known as: end of sale.

* * *

Marketing encompasses practically everything that relates to your business. And every aspect needs to be consistent. In other words- you need every word of every ad you run, every word of every brochure you send out and every piece of clothing you wear while promoting your business, to be consistent. Consistent in quality. Consistent in pricing. Consistent in style.

HEY BILL, DO YOU HAVE AN EXAMPLE?

Who in the heck did they hire to write those stupid headl...geez...I just *gave* an examp..Well, anyways...Let's look at the following illustration of the point: you're a songwriter and you write humorous songs. Consider how you'd like to come across- you want people to know you write totally hilarious tunes but you don't want them to think *you* are a joke or to be taken lightly. You decide that if you had to sum it up in a phrase, that phrase would be: I'm Joe Songwriter and I'm serious about writing funny songs.

Periodically throughout your career you should review everything in-volving your business that potential clients come in contact with and ensure each facet of your marketing, from the clothes you wear to the typesetting on your letterhead, is consistent with the phrase that sums up your business. You don't have to put your slogan on everything. You could, but often it's better to imply the slogan. How? To imply that you're a serious songwriter who writes funny songs you would need to: 1. Write truly funny songs. 2. Be serious about everything else. If you try to write funny songs but some fall a bit short, only allow the public to hear the truly funny ones. Don't dilute your efforts.

Be sure your business stationary is simple and professional. Don't write something amateurish like "Freelance Songwriter" on it. That's kind of obvious isn't it? When you submit a package to a song publisher, doesn't your demo tape of songs, with your name listed as the writer, imply that already?

In your cover letters be serious. Resist the jokes. You're not a clown; you're a serious songwriter who happens to write funny songs. Don't wear plastic noses. Don't have funny messages on your answer machine. And don't hire the clown that writes the subheads in this book to write your bio.

NO, I MEANT A *GOOD* EXAMPLE

Just ignore that idiot....Let's take a more in-depth look at another example: Your home-based Cut Rate Recording Studio is going to charge half as much as your competition: home-based Top Rate Charlie's Studio. Why would anyone come to you? Because you're cheaper of course! You can produce either CD's or cassettes just like Charlie but your main recording unit is five times better than his, and Charlie could tie a porkchop around his neck and still have trouble getting a dog to like him. Not many people dig Charlie much. You're bound to succeed right?

Probably not. First, Charlie has been in business for years. You might be better, and cheaper, but he has the customers. It will cost you a lot of money to woo the people who record at Charlie's away from him long enough to even try your studio. "Money?" you ask. "Can't I just tell everyone I know about my studio and hang a sign out?"

Not likely. You're counting on people not liking Charlie; that once they have an alternative, they'll beat your door down. Very doubtful. They may not like Charlie but his service is pretty good. You're better than Charlie but you can only prove it if the customers actually come to your studio. Getting them there will cost advertising dollars. People are creatures of habit. They're thinking... "Cut-Rate is half the price but I'm used to Charlie's. I'd rather spend $750 and get the product I'm used to, than risk wasting $400. Besides if they're so good why is the price so low? They must have junk equipment. Even their name, Cut Rate, sounds cheap."

Your sign *might* pull in a few people (it *is* consistent with your other marketing right?). But do you really know everyone else who uses recording services in the area? Will you see them all? Wouldn't a flyer mailed to them along with a series of ads in all the local papers (specifically stating the quality of your equipment and your extensive experience) be far more liable to break down their reservations and bring them to your studio with money in hand than a chance meeting at a bar or supermarket?

Forget it, you're goin' down in flames anyway

You don't own Cut-Rate Studios. Not for long at least. What you own is a business about to fail due to inconsistent marketing. Even if you pull in plenty of customers you aren't charging enough. If your equipment cost 5 times Charlie's, then you're trying to make equipment payments that are several times higher than his. You also must feed a much larger ad budget, since he's already established.

When you set your prices, you probably thought Charlie was gouging his customers. In reality you didn't understand all the costs associated with business such as phone lines, down time, repairs, insurance, and advertising. At best Charlie was making a fair profit. By charging half his rate while carrying many times his overhead, you're bound to have a negative cash flow every month. Within your first year you'll be facing the very problem that faces thousands of novice entrepreneurs every month- you run out of cash, and no one will lend you any money. Faced with no alternative you make the same decision those other thousands make: you quietly pull your ads, take down your signs, and go out of business. If you avoid bankruptcy in the process, you're lucky. Or were you smart enough to start part time?

Consistency in marketing would have prevented this situation. Had you first figured out what you had to offer that Charlie didn't- your experience plus your willingness to invest in first-rate equipment- you would have realized you were selling a higher quality service, not a lower-priced service, than Charlie. You would have then set your price higher, chose a name consistent with quality, etc. Your chances of success would have increased greatly. The way you did it, your chances of succeeding were about the same as your chances of bicycling up Mt. Everest. On a Huffy.

Marketing consistency is essential in all your dealings with customers, potential customers, suppliers and even competitors. It will help you carve out a niche in your field and increase sales. In the long run it will help you maximize profits.

CHAPTER FOUR

Self-Publishing:

Newsletters, Courses, and Books

Self-publishing is a great way to get started in writing. It will build your chops- that is, it will help you improve as a writer. It will let you avoid the rejection letters that are a part of submitting your writing to established publishers. It will let you keep <u>all</u> the profits from your writing instead of a small fraction. Plus, if your eye *is* on writing for glossy magazines and top book publishers someday... there's no reason self-publishing has to interfere with your plans. And self-publishing can help you establish writing credentials while giving you clips. Without clips, (samples of your published work "clipped" from magazines), you'll have a difficult time convincing a pro publication to assign you to write anything.

Publishing is big business. Total revenue is difficult to ascertain exactly, because many publishing businesses are privately held and jealously guard sales figures; however, publishing information is known to be at least a fifteen to twenty *billion* dollar-a-year business. And the true total is likely higher than that. Books account for approximately nine billion dollars of that amount and newsletters are credited with well over one billion dollars of it. The remainder is split between reports, courses, and other less common means of conveying information.

What is self-publishing?

Self-publishing, loosely-defined, means to take material that you write yourself and make it available to the public in published form, usually for a price. "Making it available in published form" means that you make copies of your writing or have copies made, and attempt to distribute those copies. You might decide to pay a printer to typeset the writing and print ten thousand copies, or you might simply type up your manuscript on an electric typewriter and make copies on a copy machine.

* * *

Even hand-written copy could be considered self-publishing- *if* you made copies of the original and sold it. For all practical purposes though, self-published works are usually typed or typeset and many have a combination of both typing and typesetting. Many newsletters, for example, have the logotype (the title of the newsletter) and the masthead (the public information such as subscription rates, who the publisher is, etc.) typeset, while the body (the "news" part of a newsletter) is simply typed (or composed on a computer which makes it look as if it were typed).

* * *

There are many methods you can use to produce any particular self-published work, and hundreds of combinations of those methods.

A book, for example, could be produced by having one thousand covers printed at a print shop; the headings and titles could be done on a computer by a desktop publisher; and the

Two of the author's self-published products

Right: My old love and nemesis: *The Listen Again Music Newsletter* (one issue of 48 published). It was self-published using a typewriter with built-in word processing capabities.

Left: A section of my landscape course. *Learning the Lawn Maintenance and Landscaping Business* was produced on a computer using Microsoft Publisher software then run off on a photocopier.

Both products were 81/2" x 11" and both were profitable.

bulk of the writing typed. One thousand copies of the computer/typed work could be run off on a copy machine, and the whole thing stapled at the spine. Of course the whole project could be typeset and printed, and would look more professional as a result. It all depends on what you're trying to accomplish. Many self-published works sell just fine as long as the print is readable and the *information* is sound.

Online and Electronic Publishing

E-mail newsletters, e-books, disks, CDs and other electronic forms of communication are definitely viable vehicles for the self-publisher. Since the first printing of this book, the author has published a free e-mail newsletter for songwriters (which was started with the expressed purpose of marketing the author's recording business) and a how-to-play guitar CD, an audio companion to the author's recently published *Guitar Shop* book. CD sales have been increasing steadily, while many sales have been traced directly to the newsletter. E-mail newsletters can successfully charge for subscriptions if the information is valuable enough, but for most businesses, an e-newsletter serves best as an avenue to repeatedly contact customers, increasing the chance they'll purchase.

* * *

The main difference between self-published works and works that are published by established publishers? If you undertake self-publishing, *you* assume all the financial risk of the venture. If your venture is successful, you stand to make a lot of money, if it fails, you stand to lose the money you invested. If, on the other hand, your work is published by an established, reputable publisher, you will stand only to gain, not lose. The downside to signing with a regular publisher is that if sales are moderate, often the only money you'll receive will be your advance. Given equal numbers of sales in a decent volume, you'll make far more from a self-published work.

One other type of publishing exists. This is so-called "vanity publishing." If you are approached by a vanity publisher it's best to run the other way. And run fast. Vanity publishers will publish your book, but only for a fee. And you will be the one who pays the fee.

To a desperate-to-get-published writer, a vanity publishing deal can be as tempting as chocolate cake to someone on a spinach-only diet. But if the dieter eats the cake at least he gets everything he was promised. If you sign up for a vanity deal, you'll likely receive a poor product. And once would-be buyers of your work- such as librarians, book stores and the like- see the vanity publishers name on the cover, they'll see you as "just another would-be writer suckered in by a vanity publisher" and you'll lose not only the sale, but also your credibility as an author.

* * *

If book reviewers and librarians frown on vanity publishing deals, won't they frown on a self-published book also? No. First, as long as you call your publishing company something other than your last name and do a quality job, they may not even realize they're looking at a self-published work. Second, many classic works (and many modern day bestsellers) were self-published first, then were later picked up for distribution by an established publisher.

Another big reason your self-published work will be taken seriously: while vanity publishers turn out the cheapest, fastest work possible, self-publishers are generally producing quality that comes very close to rivaling the big New York publishers. Self-publishing is seen as a respectable method of getting in print. Technology, which is constantly advancing, will only lessen the small gap that exists.

* * *

Vanity publishing houses are not to be confused with printers who specialize in publishing books. Both will print your book for a fee; however, a specialist printer will strive to do a quality job at a fair price- and that's all they'll claim to do. Vanity publishers can be recognized by their glowing evaluations of your talent, promises of lucrative royalties (that almost surely won't materialize) and vague promises of "promotion" (which probably won't be fulfilled).

Why does a market exist for self-publishing?

With all the newspapers, magazines, and books in circulation, you'd think the world would have plenty to read already. And given the choice, most people *would* buy an established newspaper or major publisher's book over a home-made effort. But major publishers only publish subjects that they believe will sell in huge volume and newspapers mostly cover hard news that appeals to a wide cross section of people.

Magazines may be targeted at a fairly segmented group, (*Sports Afield* appeals mostly to hunting and fishing enthusiasts for example) but magazines are usually profitable only if their circulation numbers are huge. There are many micro-market segments that can't be profitably served by magazines. People who enjoy hunting wild boars in the state of California probably do subscribe to a national-circulation hunting magazine but they may also buy a subscription to *California Hog Hunter* even though it's lack of advertising and limited number of subscribers force the price to $49 for just four issues. Yes, *California Hog Hunter* really exists. And yes, that's really the price. It's sister publication *Western Birds* is a whopping $100 for six issues.

There's a market for self-publishing because the established media is unable to specialize enough to satisfy everyone. To be successful in this business you must identify needs that exist

An example of two higher-priced newsletters

While these are professionally designed, remember that it's mainly the value of the information in them, rather than the quality of the paper or design that makes them valuable.

My own newsletter was typed and rarely used graphics, yet at $45 for 12 issues it enjoyed excellent renewal rates during the first three years. And that was over ten years ago.

and fill them at a price potential customers are willing and able to pay.

Will you have to relocate to self-publish successfully?

In most cases: no. Usually the opportunities exist wherever you care to live and work. If you have enough space in your home for a computer, a copy machine, and mailing supplies-you're in business. Since the composition can be done in your home, and much, if not all, of the promotion and fulfillment of the orders can be done by mail, it doesn't matter where you live. There are a few notable exceptions: Producing a newsletter about the "inside" gossip in Hollywood would probably be best done *in* Hollywood. Otherwise your "inside information" might be a re-hash of days-old stories. Likewise, if you write a course called *Learning the Virginia Pest Control Business*, at some point you need to go to Virginia and either work as an exterminator or do extensive research there.

One other thing to keep in mind: if your publication is area-specific, and it is a subscription-type publication; it would be difficult to move from that area and keep the publication going.

How difficult is it to crack this nut? And is it any easier if I'm a squirrel?

Publishing in general is highly competitive. For example: there are some 45,000-50,000 book titles published each year. Though almost half are reprints, that's still a lot of competition for space in bookstores. Small publishers must avoid direct competition with major publishers in terms of product offered and sales methods to be successful.

A self-publishing venture is not difficult to start. It *will* require a substantial investment of time and money (more on that later in this chapter). To be profitable, it's essential that you choose a niche that the established publishers are ignoring, and price your work properly.

You need to research ideas thoroughly. If you are writing a book which you intend to sell to seal hunters in Alaska for example, you should investigate things like: how many seal hunters are there in Alaska? What is their average income? Can the average seal hunter afford to pay $50 for a book? And so on. If you've picked a good niche, have a good lifetime marketing plan in place (and follow through with it); and your research and pricing are good, then your chances of turning a profit are good. And yes, cracking a nut is always easier if you're a squirrel.

* * *

It's the people who don't research the marketability of their ideas (or who do the research then ignore negative results), and the people who publish fiction, trying to compete head-to-head with famous authors and major publishing houses, who usually end up selling three books and have to store the other 9,997 in a spare bedroom forever.

* * *

Are your writing skills good enough for you to succeed in self-publishing?

Being a good writer has little to do with whether you attended journalism school or not. Many regular contributors to national magazines and many successful book authors never went to J-school. Writing well is a product of research, organizing your thoughts, expressing yourself clearly and more than anything else- rewriting your manuscript until it's the best it can be. All writers improve as they go. The more you write, the better you'll get. If you have at least three sources of professional confirmation (a friend or relative doesn't count) that you are a good writer- let's say you've had two articles published in national magazines plus you were hired to write ad copy for a local business once, then you don't need to wonder. You're good enough.

If you have no professional confirmation then you should type up a practice manuscript and rewrite it until you believe you can't make it any better; then ask a professional writer or an English teacher to review it and give you an evaluation. If your evaluation comes up short then you need to consider taking writing classes at a local college or enrolling in a writer's correspondence course.

How much money can you expect to make in self-publishing?

Books and booklets: profits in self-publishing can go as high as 40% as opposed to royalties of only 6-10% if you sign with an established publisher. Of course 40% of zero is zero. On the other hand 40% of 100,000 twenty-dollar books is nearly 1 million dollars in profits. And some writers sell even more than that. Dan Poynter, who self-publishes several books knows the ropes of doing it yourself as well as anyone. According to his book The *Self-Publishing Manual*, he's enjoyed sales of over 500,000 books during his career. Several of his titles sell steadily at the rate of 10,000 copies per year, every year.

Your income will vary depending on how many books, reports or booklets you can sell and how steadily you can sell them. Some self-publishing attempts fail miserably. Others have resulted in authors making a good steady living and in some cases, the author eventually sold enough copies to become independently wealthy.

Newsletters: Your income will depend entirely on 1. How well you saturate your universe- the group of people who are potential customers for your newsletter and 2. Whether or not the subscriptions you sell are sold at a price high enough to make a profit. The biggest mistake is to price your newsletter as if it were competing with magazines. It's not. Most newsletter publishers believe the easiest path to profits is a limited-universe, high-price, fewest-possible-issues-per-year letter as opposed to a low price/big universe letter. A few newsletters are very profitable in the 500,000 and higher subscriber range though.

* * *

If you do your marketing and pricing research well you should easily achieve the industry average, which is approximately $45,000 per year for the executive editor of a successful NL. You could, of course, earn far more than that.

* * *

<u>Courses</u>: Selling a course is different than selling books. Few books are sold successfully by two-step advertising in magazines, while courses are often sold that way. No, you won't have to learn a new dance step. Two step advertising means you use a selling approach that involves two separate steps. Rather than selling directly from a magazine ad, you ask interested people to respond with only their name and address at first, no money. In the second step, you send sales materials to that person. In those materials you give a far more detailed explanation of your course than would be possible directly in the ad copy of a magazine ad, and ask for the order.

The reason this approach works for courses is that in general, a course is priced much higher than a book is. Selling a $25 book with a two step ad, or often any ad, is a losing proposition because only a small percentage of respondents to the ad will buy. With a $600 course though, the small percentage who buy may bring in enough money to cover the ad cost plus the cost of mailing information several times to the respondents who don't buy.

Courses are expensive to develop but a well-executed course, steadily advertised in related-subject magazines, can sell steadily at a high price. The profit margins on a course can be high as well- meaning there is no limit to your potential income. But courses *can* fail- a loss of enormous amounts of time and money.

Self-publishing income is dependent on how much product you sell at a profit. How much product you sell will depend on how much planning, time, energy, and money you put into selling.

A success story

If you doubt it's possible to sell a self-published work to anyone other than your friends and family, then an article published in the Beaver County Times on Sunday January 10th, 1999 should interest you. It details the success of a book about local fisherman George Harvey. His friend Dan Shields felt George's knowledge of fly fishing was impressive enough to make a sellable book and decided to bankroll the project. Dan compiled "Memories, Patterns and Tactics" based on hours of tape recorded conversations with George. He then published it with his own money, and began selling it at $24.95 through a local shop specializing in flyfishing. A special limited edition was produced also; priced at $79.95. At the time of the article's publication, Dan reported sales of about 600 copies only a few months after the book was released.

How much money will you need to invest to start a self-publishing enterprise?

If you have access to a typewriter, then a newsletter could be typed on a six cent sheet of white paper, and 500 photocopies could be made at the local quick print for a total production investment of $25 or so (many successful NL's are only one page long). If you decided to have the logotype and headings typeset, add $15 for the printer.

It sounds like a cheap, easy business to get into... but it's not. You still have to mail out those copies so add 500 stamps, which adds nearly $200 more per issue. *The real expense though, was in finding those 500 people you're mailing to!*

You needed to do an awful lot of high quality mailings to find 500 people who would pay $50 a year for your NL (the lowest price you determined you could charge and expect a profit). How many? Well, the average response rate to an unsolicited mailing is normally about 1% and often less. So... figure you mailed to at least 5,000 people to obtain your 500 subscribers. Postage and printing alone for that mailing was in the neighborhood of $2,000. *And with 500 subscribers you're only grossing 25 thousand dollars a year!* From that $25,000 you've got a lot of overhead to cover before you see your first dollar. Clearly you need to do more of those $2,000 mailings to find more subscribers...and whew! This business is starting to get expensive!

* * *

Many people only consider how much it costs to produce a publication and forget the most expensive part- finding the people who will buy it.

You need a well-thought out plan before you start any type of self-publishing, taking into account: ad costs, promo costs, likely response rates; the costs of every facet of every mailing; the cost to fulfill your orders and how you'll finance each step. If you plan on financing the operation with profits from a preceding step, then you can't also use that same money for personal income. You'll need some other source of income to live on until your venture produces sufficient income to not just pay it's own way, but also pay for its own growth with enough resources left over for you to draw a salary.

A computer and printer are not absolute necessities to start a newsletter but it sure makes the work a lot easier. For most businesses in this book it's best to put off purchasing computer because the time involved learning to use it, and the expenses involved in buying it, maintaining it, and keeping it supplied with ink, paper, discs, backup copies, etc. are better used marketing your business. In self-publishing; however, a computer will get constant use and is worth the trouble and expense. You should definately figure one into your start-up costs.

How long will it take to see your first check?

Writing speed varies from person to person, and of course a 280 page book takes a lot longer to produce than a 30 page booklet. Part of your planning will entail estimating how quickly you can write the manuscript. The other part is calling your printer (unless your product is totally homemade) to see how fast he can produce it.

We'll assume the printing of your first order of product is completed. The method you use to sell the product will then determine how long it takes to get a check in hand. These are the most common methods of selling self-published works:

- In-person sales at bookstores Don't try to set up an autograph party until you have some product in hand, just in case there are delays. Then figure at least one month before you can realistically set up a party and have time to promote it successfully. Depending on your agreement with the store, you may get your first check that day.

- Consignment sales Leaving a few copies at various stores on consignment often moves product. Set up regular collections and servicing of your consignment accounts weekly. You should be able to get your first check the second week, providing you had sales. You may only sell a few copies a month at each store so contact a lot of stores.

- Paid ads in publications You may wish to start running certain ads far in advance of having product. Orders from newspapers can arrive just a few days after placing a classified but magazines will generally take at least two and a half months. Some magazines have ad deadlines so far prior to the publication date that six months will pass before you could possibly have your first order in hand.

- <u>Rented mailing lists</u> These lists are sold by various companies that are comprised of the names of people who are (hopefully) prime targets for your offer. Lists of mail order buyers, book buyers, high-income homeowners, and more are available. Rent a productive list using a credit card and you could have orders in hand within two weeks.

- <u>Internet sales</u> The Internet is more difficult to sell on than you might be led to believe by the media and others. Unless you get top placement in search engines or your product is moveable via online auctions you may have a difficult time moving anything anytime but if you accept credit cards, *in theory* you could slap up a page and get paid that very day.

How long will it take to become established?

If you can start with enough capital to go full time your first year, you could be established- turning a profit and making a self-sustaining income- by the beginning of your second year. Some publishers have progressed to an established condition faster than that but they are the exception.

If you start part-time with a plan of plowing your profits back into the business to achieve growth, figure two to five years to become established, minimum.

Becoming an expert is something else again. Figure a minimum of ten years before you've mastered this field. If you have successfully run some other type of business, especially a creativity-required one, figure five to seven years before you will qualify as an expert.

Although some people have multi-faceted careers crossing into several fields, it's best to attempt to master one field at a time. If self-publishing is going to be your profession, spend as much time as possible learning about each aspect of publishing that you'll be involved in. Don't waste time learning things you'll be delegating to others.

Training May Be Helpful

Before start-up learn as much as possible about marketing, selling, and small business management. Both general and publishing-specific education in all three of those subjects will be helpful. Consider books; private instruction; newsletters; mail order and local college courses as sources of that information. If money is a problem, books are the cheapest method of gaining an education.

* * *

My view on investing in books:

I particularly enjoy reading how-to business books. I buy a lot of them, perhaps twenty or thirty a year. Even though some have nearly identical titles, each author brings a new viewpoint to the subject and each author almost always has some little tip or tidbit that no one else has covered. Somewhere down the road you'll use that tip to make money or save money. Occasionally you'll get a truly useless book but that's easily made up for by the winners. Almost every business-related, how-to book or course will save or make you money equivalent to many times the cover price. I've never really spent a dime on books although I invest several hundred dollars a year in them.

* * *

What sells and what doesn't?

Two broad categories most book self-publishers try to avoid are fiction and poetry as they are very difficult to sell on a small scale. Although some self-publishers have indeed carved a niche for themselves in these fields, it is highly recommended that you consider other areas if profit is your goal.

Any type of regional or county where-to book is a potential steady seller. For example: if you want to ride bike trails in Colorado, you likely won't find a book by a major publisher on the subject. There are several by small publishers though. These are books that can sell at a steady level for many years.

Books on fitness, health and self-help can sell very well. In-depth books on specific hobbies will move also. Thomas Pedigo, who self-publishes a report called "How to Win a Pinewood Car Derby," (available from The Winning Edge 4115 Cougar Place, Colorado Springs, CO 80918-5677) says in another of his booklets that the pinewood derby booklets "sell like crazy during the winter months." Pinewood Derbys are contests for boys who build toy cars out of wood and race them. Who buys the booklets? Mostly the fathers of derby entrants.

Subjects that work for books also work for booklets and reports.

Courses sell best if they are specifically geared to improving the buyer's income. Buy almost any national magazine, look at the ads for mail-order courses, and you'll quickly get the idea. Courses exist on subjects as diverse as electronics repair, taxidermy, and accounting. You might choose a popular subject and attempt to compete head to head with the established firms like NRI or ICS.

You can be successful if you either match their quality in every aspect or charge less. Just be careful you're not pricing your product so low that you can't make a profit. Advertising in magazines is expensive! Another tactic: advertise where the big firms don't. Classified or space ads in local papers can be effective. During your planning stage remember this: the average person sees an ad 12 times before they respond.

Perhaps a niche course- something few others know about and no one else is teaching- could be your key to success. There are people selling short courses, reports, and booklets on all types of things. One booklet that's been successfully sold for years is called Growbiz. It teaches people how to make plant containers out of portland cement and sell them.

How-to products of all types are a good choice, especially if they teach the reader a skill that will improve their income. And they're even more likely to sell if they are about a subject a large publisher would avoid. If you could write a book titled "How You Can Make Road-Killed Deer Pies and Earn $75,000 a Year Selling Them" you'd have a winning title. But don't write such a book unless 1. You know how to make a darn good road-killed deer pie and 2. *Have* actually made $75,000 in one year selling them. Dishonesty or stretching the truth will ruin you in the long run. Buyers won't buy again or may even return the books. You could end up in legal trouble and you won't sleep well.

You need to be well-rested for your marketing efforts so write honestly.

* * *

THE WORD ON NL'S (newsletters)

Get into the paid subscription newsletter business for one of two reasons - to make a profit, or to further your writing career. Don't jump into this expensive business just because you're in love with the idea of doing a NL or in love with a particular subject. Choose your subject based on testing, testing, and more testing! If you can't find suitable mailing lists for rent: you may not have a marketable idea. Choose a market segment, rent a list, and do a test mailing. If it fails, do not proceed. Re-think your subject.

Business NL's- such as a NL for some aspect of the automobile industry- are excellent choices. Business customers can write off the cost of the subscription and will likely see a $300 per year subscription price as a wise investment. Business people are *happy* to pay to have their news cut down in size so they spend less time keeping up with new developments. It won't be exactly easy to sell a high price NL. But when you make the sale you're likely to have that customer year after year for a long time.

Consumer newsletters- geared to the average Joe consumer- *can* work. But most consumers, used to equating value with volume, will see your $50 subscription price for 6 issues of 6 pages and compare that with a 60-page magazine they buy for under $2 an issue and balk. The answer is *not* to drop your price! You can't! Why? Did you forget how expensive those mailings are? The ones you *must* do to get new customers? You either need to convince people to pay what you need to charge or face the fact that this particular NL was a poor choice. Drop it, and move on to a different market.

TAKE IT FROM ME....

Remember when I said reading books about your profession will save you money? Had I only known *before* I founded the Listen Again Music Newsletter what I found out 5 years later while reading "Publishing Newsletters" by Howard Penn Hudson. Right on page 13, and written in very easily-readable type it basically says: Never start a "how-to" newsletter. I boiled down the actual wording for effect but that's what Howard is trying to get across.

Now you might wonder why he'd say something like that. Wouldn't people pay for good how-to advice on a particular field?

I can tell you from experience: yes, they sure will. Three years into my newsletter business I had steady subscribers with renewals near 100%. I was definitely on my way to becoming independently wealthy. Except for one little problem...

At first it wasn't a big deal, temporary writer's block I thought, I'll make up for this weak issue next month. And next month *was* a little better. But overall month by month, issue by issue, quality was declining. And my renewal rate, which is where a NL publisher makes his profit, was dropping.

Finally I had to face reality- I was running out of material! There's only so much you can teach people on a subject before you run out of fresh material, and in 1991, I was running out fast!

There was only one solution- you can't sell people one thing then give them something else. I had to shut down my NL and offer people their choice of backissues or a refund.

It was embarrassing, costly and disappointing to say the least. And it could have been avoided. Yeah, Howard's first

"Publishing Newsletters" was out in 1982, five years before I made my big mistake! And I knew the book existed, I was just too cheap to buy it! I saved twenty bucks... and cost myself a fortune! OK... that's the story. And unless you want to sit through it again: never EVER ask me why I buy so many books every year!

Pricing Your Work

In self-publishing, pricing your work is a bit easier than in some other creative fields. Ignore major publisher prices- they have volume discounts you can't hope to match. A starting point can be established by researching what similar work produced by several *competing small publishers* costs. If your work has an exceptionally small universe of potential subscribers, it must be priced higher, since you can't move as many copies. Also, the more valuable the information, the higher the price. Remember this: There's no limit to how high you can price your work, but there's a limit to what a customer will pay for it. One effective pricing method is to start on the high side, then if you can't move product, begin offering discounts.

* * *

Researching in order to determine the size of your potential market is the key. If I had written a small-universe book for a high-income group, "Advanced Ostrich Toenail Surgery for North American Veterinarians," for example, I might start with a $300 per copy book price and work down from there, if necessary. That's very reasonable for such a specialized topic. For "9 Creativity-Required Businesses You Can Start From Home," the universe was of a reasonable size, so the book was priced accordingly. If you *were* willing to pay $300 for this book, feel free to send me the difference.

My experience with self-publishing

Though my newsletter eventually ran out of gas so to speak, the experience of writing and editing those 48 issues launched my writing career. Later, I published a course called "Learning the Landscape and Lawn Maintenance Business," which turned a profit within the first year and which I still sell.

Even though my work now gets accepted regularly by established publishers, I still publish some of my writing myself: If I have an easy-to sell-to market or a built-in group of customers, the best choice is to self-publish. If I'm writing a work I want complete control over, or an idea I believe in that's been rejected by traditional publishers, the *only* choice is to self-publish.

When you do self-publish, create the highest quality product you can possibly afford. It always pays in the long run. I'll have more to say on this subject in later chapters.

It's important to keep in mind that you could *lose* money on your first project then make it up later as you add multiple products in specific categories, since your marketing should then be more efficient.

For Further Study:

The following 4 titles are available from Creative Books:

The Complete Guide to Self-Publishing by Tom & Marylin Ross. Current advice on all aspects of book publishing and marketing from production to publicity. $21.50

Making Money Writing Newsletters by Elaine Floyd. How to set up and run a newsletter production service. Includes 39 forms you can copy and use. $31.50

Jump Start Your Book Sales- A Money-Making Guide for Authors and Publishers. Includes dozens of real-life success stories. *$21.50*

Designing Direct Mail that Sells by Sandra J. Blum. Blum spills secrets she learned during 22 years of direct mail work. Includes test mailing techniques. $31.50

Orders for the above 4 titles should be sent to:

Creative Books
P. O. Box 463
Beaver, PA 15009-0463

Check or money order only. Money orders are faster. PA residents must include 6% sales tax. Prices include shipping and handling and the most recent edition in print will be shipped. Should a price increase occur, you will be notified (or send extra and the overpayment will be refunded). Allow 3-4 weeks for delivery.

Other resources:

Books In Print: R.R. Bowker & Co. 121 Chanlon Rd., New Providence, NJ 07974. All books that publishers have filed a standard ABI form on are listed in this publication. Many libraries carry it.

Newsletters In Print, Gale Research, INC, 645 Griswold St., Penobscot Bldg. Detroit, Mich. 48226. 313-961-6083. Annual Directory.

Howard Penn Hudson, who publishes the respected *Newsletter on Newsletters* wrote a very informative book on the subject titled *Publishing Newsletters* available from: MacMillan Publishing, 866 Third Ave., New York, NY 10022.

"The Self-Publishing Manual" by Dan Poynter. Carried by many libraries. A well-written book on self-publishing that is in fact, self-published. Hey, any book that's in its eighth printing is a proven product. You can find it at:

http://www.parapublishing.com

Libraries are rich sources of information on *how* to write. But avoid titles that are too general or non-specific to the type of writing you wish to do. Writing a magazine article requires a different approach than writing a research paper. Note too that library books are usually older editions and may contain out-of-date information.

A great example of a self-published book is Metal Detecting Advice & Tips, co-authored by Joe Patrick and Robert Sickler. Even if you have no interest in the subject, it's a very well done book and I recommend purchasing a copy for study before you try publishing your own book or booklet. Contact: Robert Sickler 4291 Atwood Rd. Stone Ridge, NY 12484.

NRI Schools, 4401 Connecticut Ave. NW, Washington, DC 20078-3543 offers mail-order courses in both desktop publishing and nonfiction writing.

California Hog Hunter and Western Birds can be contacted at P.O. Box 9007, San Bernadino, CA 92427-0007 or call 909-887-3444.

CHAPTER FIVE

Photography:

General and Wildlife

Pick up your phone book, turn to the yellow pages and look up "photographers." Unless you live in a very remote area you'll find at least a few listings for professional photographers. If you live in a big city, there are probably hundreds. How can so many photographers afford to run expensive ads in the yellow pages year after year? Because they are making money.

Review any local paper, national magazine or sales catalog. Someone made money taking those photos. And here's something you may not know: many of the people who take the highest-paid types of pictures are not staff photographers. They're self-employed freelancers. Why couldn't you be one of them?

What is photography?

Nearly everyone knows that photography is the capturing of images onto a permanent or semi-permanent storage medium (usually film but increasingly by storing it digitally). But in this book we're talking about making money from those captured images so perhaps the question should be: What is the difference between taking pictures and taking professional pictures?

Rather than delve into technical theories, let's cut to the quick- Pro photographers shoot in pro formats, the most common being 35 millimeter, which is usually written as 35mm. There are other pro formats but not one of them is the typical consumer-use camera. If you don't set your own shutter speed and f-stop (aperture size) before shooting the picture, your camera may not be real useful for pro photography. There are some good auto-focus 35mm's out there, some capable of taking quality photos. But *most* pro photographers prefer a camera that allows them the luxury of installing interchangeable lenses as-needed and "bracketing" pictures (shooting one f-stop 30-50% above, and one f-stop 30-50% below normal to get just the right exposure.) Most cameras that fit the bill start in the $400 range. That's without a lens.

The other main differences between pro and amateur photographers: 1. As a pro you take a lot more shots of the subject 2. You spend far more time attempting to get just the right shot.

* * *

Perhaps you need a photo of a bridge. As a pro you won't just click off a picture and walk away. You may spend a great deal of time finding various angles until the bridge is artistically "framed" by trees, then wait for dusk to capture the bridge in a beautiful sunset.

Or maybe you need a shot of a football player. You won't take one shot-you'll take many rolls of film hoping for that one picture that captures exactly the feel of the moment or style of the player you wish to portray.

The January '99 issue of *National Wildlife* magazine contains the winning entries in the *National Wildlife* photo contest. Read the short captions that accompany each entry and you'll see comments that reflect the thinking of a serious outdoor photographer. One winner built a structure to channel a raccoon to a certain spot where he could get the photo he wanted. Another entrant went through an entire roll of film in minutes in an attempt to get a certain shot of a praying mantis. Yet another spent hours in a cramped blind during a heavy snowstorm photographing birds until he felt he had a winning photo. That's the kind of dedication to craft you need to succeed in this competitive business.

* * *

Instant Pictures

No doubt, they look clear to you but instant prints and such don't reproduce well in magazines. Editors won't touch them unless there is no other possible pic available that will fit the story and that photo is a must-have. Otherwise they'll delete the pic or buy a stock photo from a stock photo company. Don't waste your time trying this business without a professional camera.

Why does a market for photography exist? Haven't there been enough photos taken?

There have been a lot of photos taken in this world and many of them are very useable. However, each day the existing photos age. Some deteriorate. Some are lost or destroyed. New technology emerges. Things are discovered. And people do new things.

10,000 high quality whale photos may exist on this planet but if a new film which gives 2% sharper images or 1% better color saturation comes on the market, then those pictures are obsolete as far as wildlife magazines that pursue top quality photos are concerned.

Also, every picture is unique. Perhaps you can photograph a whale with a certain look in its eye and under certain weather conditions that is unlike anything captured previously.

And remember, just because those ten thousand whale pictures exist, none of them may be on an editor's desk at the moment they need a whale photo. If yours is- and the quality is acceptable- you just made a sale. In creative businesses, production is only about 20% of being successful. Marketing is 80%.

Another good example is wedding photography. Every wedding is a unique, important event in the participant's lives. They want pictures and they don't want Aunt Emma's 1950 Brownie that double exposes every other picture to take them. They want a reliable pro. What it costs is what it costs.

A market for top-quality photos exist because people like to record events; to revisit memorable things through photographs; and see places, things and people they may never be able to see any other way. And they are willing to pay money for that privilege.

Wildlife Photography

If your idea of a great job would be to travel the world on assignment from glossy magazines, taking pictures of wildlife all over the world then you have a small problem. Those jobs exist but they are so rare that you may as well consider them non-existent. Most glossy magazines buy photos from stock photo agencies who buy them from freelancers. Or the magazines deal directly with the freelancers. Photographers who travel the world generally pay for the trips themselves,

35mm slides

When you put film in a camera, regular film and slide film look basically the same. What you get back is quite different. You can't simply look at a slide and see the image as you can with a photo. To see a slide you must illuminate it. They can be difficult to get used to but the increase in quality is worth the effort.

recouping their costs when the pictures sell. If you do get an occasional paid travel assignment, see it as icing on the cake.

There are several differences between wildlife and other types of photography. Long lenses, often used in many types of photography, are a must in this field. Wildlife photographers use expensive 300mm and up lenses (which attach to the 35mm camera) so that they can obtain "closeups" from a distance. Also, to be a successful wildlife or nature photographer you need to use pro-quality "slide film" for your photos to get serious consideration.

When transferred to a printed page, slides are much clearer than prints which is why many magazines, not just nature or wildlife magazines, demand them. But in general, wildlife and nature markets are the most consistently insistent. Almost all the higher paid markets for outdoor and wildlife work prefer reviewing slides, also known as transparencies.

When your slide film comes back from the lab you won't get prints, you'll receive little square frames instead. To view them you'll need a loupe and light table. It will take some getting use to. Another difference: shooting wildlife takes extreme patience. If you wouldn't be happy sitting in a blind located in the wilderness all day, and perhaps not even having one good picture to show for it, this may not be your bag. Wildlife doesn't always show up where and when you expect it to.

Where are the opportunities for photography?

The worst thing you can do when starting a photography career is to spend money on travel or relocation. Horror stories abound of beginning photographers who immediately invest in four-wheel drive vehicles, campers, top-notch equipment and quit their jobs to travel the world taking photos. Six months later, deeply in debt and with no cash flow, they start unloading

A Substitute Light Table

If you can't afford a table and loupe to view your slides this setup will get you started. A piece of white paper draped over a light substitutes as the table, while your 50 mm lens will be the substitute loupe. Put the frame of the lens close to your eye socket and peer through it as if you were the camera. Hold the slide a few inches above the "light table" then adjust the lens and slide distance until the picture is in focus and you'll see your slides in a whole new light.

stuff cheap and start looking for a job. It can take you longer than 6 months just to learn how to use your equipment properly, let alone sell pictures and get paid for them!

* * *

There are potential money making photo opportunities right where you live. If a person lives in Iowa for instance, they'd be incorrect to assume they must travel to photograph tigers or celebrities or pro football players. For one thing those subjects may be more approachable at the zoo, or a concert, or while in town for a local radio talk show.

It would be wise for the photographer to consider starting with birds rather than tigers. Or Local Johnny and the Pebbles rather than the Rolling Stones. Or high school rather than pro games. Or enter the lucrative portrait and wedding photo market.

Later, *after* learning how to take excellent pictures, and *after* steady cash flow is coming in, our novice Iowa shutterbug can begin to branch out. First with short trips, then working up to the longer ones, supported by sales of photos every step of the way.

* * *

How hard is it to break into this business?

It's highly competitive. You must be able to take technically flawless pictures of course. And you must be able to "edit" well which is another way of saying: toss the bad pics in a garbage can and attempt to sell only your best work. That being said, the wedding and portrait markets are easier to get started in. Ads placed in local papers, yellow page ads, and direct mail to organizations and businesses that might need pics can all be effective forms of advertising your service. Be sure to give them time to work.

Newspapers, catalog work, magazines, and books are difficult markets. Generally: the more glamorous the work, the more competitive it is. But even for glossy magazine work, your photos won't really be competing with freelancers who have 100,000 slides in their collection. Or stock agencies with far more than that. Sure they have that many but it's common sense: editors aren't going to review 100,000 slides to fill a space. They'll look at a few photos from each potential source.

* * *

Magazine work is competitive but you can break in much easier by doing five things:

1. Start with very small circulation magazines and work your way up.

2. Market aggressively.

3. Learn to write. Stories with pictures sell much easier than photos alone.

4. Constantly build your stock of photos. Magazines will eventually put you on their list of photographers who receive "want" lists- lists of photos they need for upcoming issues. The more pictures you have, the more likely you'll have something to submit.

5. Know the publication thoroughly. The best way to do that is to subscribe, then study the photos and stories they print each month.

* * *

A word about advertising: This applies to all businesses (which is why you should read this entire book- otherwise you'll miss these little gems). There's a misconception among many would-be entrepreneurs that stops more business start-ups dead in their tracks than any other factor.

The misconception is that advertising is supposed to "make you money." In the long run, yes, it's supposed to put dollars in your pockets. But don't make the mistake of thinking an ad that cost you $150 and only brought you in $50 in business is a mistake.

Ads almost never make money directly. Rather *they are the catalyst that gets the money making process started.* You might run a $150 ad every month for 6 months. And each time it runs it brings in $50. You grossed

$300 and spent $900. You're losing money right? Technically, yes. But should you pull the ad and find something else to do with your life? Probably not.

If you have a quality product or service you need to ask yourself- are the customers who spent the $300 likely to be repeat customers? Were they so happy with what they received for their money that they'll recommend the product or service to a friend who will likely purchase it someday?

If you can honestly answer yes to either question, then you should keep advertising. As the customers begin coming back and/or telling their friends who then become customers, your business will slowly begin to grow. Because your ad is continuing you'll keep adding new customers. Word of mouth will soon be adding more. Almost like a pyramid scheme (except this is honest) your business will grow. When business triples you'll break even ($900 out and $900 in) and time will become your friend. The amount of money you're putting out for the ad will stay the same but each month the amount you take in will grow. And as long as you can service the new customers with a quality product or service, the growth will likely continue.

You've surely heard the phrase "most businesses lose money their first year or two." It's true. And the reason is because it can take that long for the income to catch up with the cost of the advertising, start-up costs and overhead.

With most small home businesses you don't have a great deal of ongoing overhead which is a huge advantage. Still you do normally have at least some money invested to get started. If advertising is part of your marketing plan you must allow it time to work its magic.

* * *

How can I have my photographic work evaluated?

If your photos are selling then your work has already been evaluated.... and you passed the test. But if they aren't- you're getting rejection slips or can't seem to get hired to do a simple wedding- is it lack of experience? Your failure to use enough deodorant? The sample photos your five-year-old used as a substitute coloring book? Or simply the fact that your printer gave you 80% off on your business cards- an irresistible deal-except where it should say "Digital Photographer" it says "Pigital Dotographer?"

Good reasons all, but what you need to know is: is it the pictures themselves?

Editors are normally too busy to bother with making comments on your submissions. To end the catch-22 you're caught in, you need to find someone experienced enough to evaluate them correctly. A local solution is to either 1. Ask the local photo shop that develops your pictures to give you a few tips. 2. Ask a local reputable photographer for comments. It's worth a try but they may be too busy or hedge on an honest evaluation to avoid hurting your feelings or avoid losing your business. Joining a local photography club is another possibility, though you may learn more by osmosis than a direct evaluation.

You could also enroll in a photography class. Of course that is an expensive method and it will take time to get answers, but if your pics are not quite pro-level, you will receive the help you need to correct any problems.

* * *

A Success Story

Tony Rath was involved in photography for 14 years before turning pro and has certainly seen his share of success. Although he now divides his time between photography and his Internet company, his camera work provided him with a full-time living from 1992 to 1996.

Noted for his outdoor, natural light, and underwater work, the high point of his career to date has been a five-week-long photo assignment for the World Wildlife Fund in Oaxaca, Mexico. During that trip, he realized the importance of computerizing his stock and suggests that beginners start a computerized filing system early in their career.

He definitely recommends photography as a profession "if the person has ambition, is healthy and physically strong, likes to travel, and enjoys working alone."

Tony feels a photographer should "look for pictures even when they don't have a camera in their hand." And "should learn how to reply graciously when someone praises their work, but don't believe them." Particularly insightful is his view that if you have enough photographs to run a stock photo business, you might wish to consider putting up an Internet Web Page. "The Internet is definitely changing the way stock photography is done as a good percentage of my annual sales are directly attributable to marketing on the Internet," he says.

Of course it takes more than just a few handfuls of photos to pull this off. Tony's stock is in the vicinity of five thousand images and many photographers have ten or twenty times that amount in their personal stock.

His advice to anyone thinking of seriously pursuing photography as a business? "Shoot, shoot, shoot, and shoot some more."

How much money will you need to invest to start?

Figure at least $500 for a good camera and 50mm lens setup. Sports and wildlife photographers should consider adding a zoom lens with at least 300mm capability, and will still yearn for higher power magnification. There are a lot of accessories that can be added as you go such as tripods, filters, a screen for portrait work, and the like. And keep in mind: there's a lot of good used equipment on the market. Even if you go with new stuff, $600-750 should get you started.

Marketing your work is another cost to consider. Don't sink thousands of dollars into a two month ad blitz or a package mailing frenzy unless you can sustain that level of intensity...It's far better to spend $500 running a small $10 ad for 50 weeks than to spend $500 on a quarter page add for one week. As long as your name is consistently out there, you're building a business.

The same goes for mailing out packages to magazines. Spending $5 a week for years, is far, far better than blowing even $1,500 in one shot, being disappointed with the results, and losing faith. Plus, consider that *two years from now you will likely be taking much better pics and definitely have a much bigger catalog* to choose from.

But don't take that idea to the extreme either and "delay" your marketing. Choose an amount you can easily afford and use it to market consistently, year in-year out.

A big ongoing cost will be in film. You're going to have bad shots and you're going to make mistakes. Many professionals consider obtaining one useable picture per roll as doing great. Figure about fifty cents to a dollar each time you click the shutter for the film and developing costs. For beginners who aren't getting any sales yet, the negative cash flow due to film alone can damper their enthusiasm quickly.

* * *

Clicking pictures all day is fun, no doubt about it. And as a new photographer you do need pics to build a catalog and gain experience. But until you start getting jobs or selling pics, it's impractical to spend all your financial resources on film. Here's the solution:

Set an affordable limit to your clicking in terms of rolls. If you can afford only one or two rolls a week, then that's your limit. Don't exceed it. You'll still build a quality catalog...slowly.

☞ Spend most of your shooting time setting up quality shots rather than burning through your rolls quickly.

☞ Don't forget the 80/20 rule: For every hour you spend creating the product (taking pics, buying film, and having it developed) spend 4 hours marketing your work or service. If you break that rule at all, break it by doing extra marketing, not taking pics.

☞ There's really no excuse for wasting time. You can always make up sales flyers, make up packages (even if you lack stamp money right now) search for new markets, network, go to the library and study magazines, read and re-read books, etc. There are plenty of low and no-cost things you can do to propel your career ahead.

* * *

As you can see, photography can be expensive during the start-up phase. But it doesn't have to be *ridiculously* expensive. The photographer who spends *time-* targeting the marketing and choosing quality shots- may actually see success faster than if they had "blitzed" the market.

When will that first check come?

Marketing yourself locally as a general photographer, you could conceivably run an ad, get a job, and have a check in your hand within two weeks.

Print media pay two main ways: 1. "On acceptance," which actually can mean anything from a few days after they accept your work for publication, to 30 or even 60 days later, or 2. They pay "on publication." And there are photographers who claim they've waited as long as 7 years for a particular photo to be published.

Fortunately that's not the norm. Publication is normally sometime within the first year after acceptance. Maybe the very next month. Once a piece is published you may receive your check a few days later, or up to 60 days later.

How long does it take to become an established photographer?

From the day you take your first picture with the intention of turning pro, until you have a self-sustaining business that fully supports you- figure anywhere from one to three years if you are starting a freelance wedding or portrait business, though some photographers reach that point much faster.

Magazine photography will take longer partly because the wheels turn slowly at most publications. Extra slow at the large circulation markets that pay exceptionally well.

Consider too that with magazine work, after your photos are accepted it can be months before your work is actually printed and released to the public. *Outdoor Life* states in their writer's guidelines that they are normally working one *year* in advance. Writer's guides are 1-4 pages of text available at most publications for a stamped self-addressed envelope (normally abbreviated to SASE). With lead times like that, it can take a while for you to develop a name for yourself or even to build a catalog of credentials and clips. Figure three to five years to become established. Ten years minimum to qualify as an expert.

How much can you expect to make?

It depends a lot on you- the quality of pictures you take, the reputation you develop, how aggressively you market, and how many people you have under you to pay. If you do poorly at those things you might make under $5,000 per year. But the average serious photographer can normally expect to see $20,000 - $50,000 net per year. The very best photographers who are excellent at marketing, business building, or getting their photos placed with stock agencies have virtually unlimited income potential.

* * *

Help is expensive and more than anything else will either cut your profit substantially or help you make more. If you can work 4 or 5 weddings on a Saturday, each grossing $2,500 by hiring other photographers, it would likely push profits up. If you are going to Africa and take a helper to lug equipment and provide moral support, that's probably just an extra expense. Most pro photographers do take help on location then make it pay by having the hired person catalog pictures, keep extensive notes for caption writing later, etc;

freeing the photographer to shoot more pictures, thus having a higher potential gross from pictures taken during the trip.

* * *

Pricing Your Work

Detailed pricing is far beyond the scope of this book; however, the following will give you a general idea of how to figure it out.

For wedding and portrait photography, call several of your competitor's ads in the yellow pages asking for prices on both. That will give you a grasp of what goes in your area. Follow-up with a drive by of each shop. If the prices are from studios with regular business locations, you may be able to charge slightly less since you have less overhead starting from home.

Fortunately, publications usually tell *you* what they're willing to pay when they call to accept the work, a much more comfortable situation for the photographer. They usually say something like "This is Donna Editor from New Photo Magazine, we like the leaf picture you sent and want to use it in our October issue. We can pay $250 for a quarter page."

It's unlikely they'll attempt to underpay you. Nearly all publications have writer's guides and often separate photographer's guides available that include specific pay rates. You should write to publications long before you intend to submit anything, requesting both guides so you'll know in advance what to expect. Don't forget the SASE or your request will go straight to the wastebasket.

***

Here's a good point to keep in mind: John Shaw who is a highly successful nature photographer, says his income increased dramatically the year he began submitting text along with his pictures. In his book *The*

Business of Nature Photography, he highly recommends submitting photo essay ideas in the form of queries. Pictures alone are harder for an editor to place.

* * *

Not all publications accept freelance work and it's far too costly to start researching which ones do on your own. To break into newspapers, newsletters, magazines, books, greeting cards, trade journals, stock agencies and other less obvious markets, you should purchase two "must have" books: Writer's Market, and Photographer's Market (both are available from Creative Books or at your local chain bookstore.) Between the two they list over 6,000 places to sell your text and/or photos. And the listings are quite detailed as to what each listing pays.

You'll find that most rates are acceptable. And some are more than that. Many cover shots pay over $1,000 for one picture. And that may be only for the right to use it one time. After publication you are then free to sell that same picture elsewhere.

For Further Study:

The following five titles are available from Creative Books. This first book, as mentioned two paragraphs ago, is a "must have":

Photographer's Market. This is an annual (the most recent edition will be sent). Detailed listings of 2,000 places to sell your photographs. $25.50.

Writer's Market. (Revised annually. The most recent edition will be sent.) Many photographers believe this is just as much of a must-have as *Photographer's Market* because it's often easier to sell photos with a story. 8,000 editors who buy what you write. And most of them buy photos too. $29.50.

The Professional Photographer's Guide to Shooting and Selling Nature and Wildlife Photos. Just what the title says it is. $26.50.

Sell & Re-sell your photos. The bible on marketing photos. Filled with example photos, helpful charts, tables, and sidebars. $18.50.

The Photographer's Market Guide to Photo Submissions and Portfolio Formats. Detailed, visual examples guide you through the photo submission and selling maze to maximize income from your images. $20.50.

All of the five books above are available by sending a check or money order for the price of the books desired, plus $1.50 shipping per book to:

Creative Books
P.O. Box 463
Beaver, PA 15009-0463

Check or money order only (Money orders receive priority delivery). Prices include shipping and handling and the most recent edition in print will be shipped. Should a price increase occur, you will be notified (or send extra and the overpayment will be refunded). Add $10 for Canadian orders. Allow 2-4 weeks for delivery.

John Shaw's *The Business of Nature Photography*, a well-written book by a respected pro photographer, is available from:

Amphoto Books
Watson-Guptill Publications
1515 Broadway
New York, NY 10036

Many universities and colleges throughout the world offer courses in photography. Check your local library for *Peterson's Guide to Four-Year Colleges.*

Most public libraries have a fairly extensive photography section. The titles may be dated so try to retain only the "timeless" information (advice on composition and similar topics). Ignore discussions of the latest or best equipment, pricing your work, etc.

Tony Rath can be contacted at Tony Rath Photography, Box 216, Danigra, Belize. If you need photos or wish to view a pro photographer's work, visit his website: http://www.trphoto.com.

As this section is being revised for the second printing, major dot coms are failing in droves, so offering specific Internet addresses is risky, but if you choose a major search engine and type in *photography business* and you can quickly locate dozens of sites offering free information.

There are numerous professional organizations photographers can join such as:

The International Center of Photography

ph: (212) 860-1781,

The Photographic Society of America
ph: (405) 843-1437

Wedding and Portrait Photographers International
ph: (310) 451-0090

North American Nature Photography Association
ph: (303) 422-8527

* * *

Chapter 6

Landscaping

Landscaping is everywhere. Drive through any suburban area and you can't help but notice the beautiful plants, rocks, timbers, waterfalls, and other elements that add beauty to residential and commercial properties. Those landscapes were designed by a landscape architect, a landscaper, or the homeowner; then they were installed by a landscaper or homeowner.

Installing a landscape can be hard work- especially without the right tools. With the right tools and the right weather- it is truly a joyful task. And designing or installing landscapes is extremely profitable, plus it's in big demand in most areas.

There are several ways to learn this intriguing business including going to college to obtain a degree in horticulture. But you can make plenty of money in landscaping without a degree and you don't necessarily have to do any labor either. If you are good at finding customers, designing the landscape and selling the job; you can subcontract the actual work to an experienced crew.

What is landscaping?

Landscaping is best defined as intentionally beautifying outdoor areas of a property. It principally encompasses removing old, worn out plantings and/or adding new trees or shrubs. Sometimes it involves grading soil or installing decorative elements such as crushed stone.

The design and selling phase entails advertising your service; responding to the phone inquiry; meeting with the customer; taking pictures and measurements of the site; discussing the customers needs; and then designing the job to the customers satisfaction.

The installation phase encompasses scheduling the job; planning the progression of the work; arranging for supplies to be picked up or delivered to the jobsite at the appropriate time; going to a nursery to pick out the shrubs, trees, and perennials needed; and going to a bulk landscape supplier to choose rock, mulch, and other supplies; then installing all of the preceding items in a professional, timely manner.

Why does a market exist for landscaping?

People have many motives for wanting a nice landscape such as to "outdo the neighbors," to improve property values or because local codes might require a certain level of landscaping, but mostly: landscaping improves the look of a property and people want their property to look its best. And businessmen know an attractive property increases sales and enhances their image.

When old landscapes outlive their usefulness or new properties are developed, the need to install a new landscape is created. While some people attempt the job themselves, most prefer to hire someone to do the work because they don't have access to the suppliers and equipment or because they lack experience and know that a professional landscaper will likely do a better job and create a landscape that is much more useable and valuable. Often, in the long run, it's simply cheaper to hire a landscaper.

Where are the opportunities?

Landscaping opportunities exist throughout the western, eastern, northern, and southern United States, though it may not be booming in your particular area. Like photography, you can give landscaping the phone book test. If there are quite a few landscapers listed in the yellow pages of your phone book, the opportunity exists for you to capture some of the market they're serving. The best areas are usually ones with a lot of new developments that cater to higher income homeowners.

Do some research- talk to local nursery owners, explain you're thinking of getting into the business and ask if many landscapers buy plants there. Landscapers are potential prime customers so a nursery owner will be quite happy to talk to you about the local landscape business and will probably have some tips on where to find "hot", booming areas.

Often a certain area comprised of older, medium and low income homes is slow for landscape work but a few miles away there is a booming area that will support your business. Many companies are successful in older-home areas by combining landscape maintenance and grass cutting with installation. We'll get deeper into that subject later in the chapter.

If there are few opportunities for landscaping in your area, you may need to relocate to the nearest large city or to a southern state where the work is year-round. Georgia and Florida are just two of the many southern states where opportunities for landscapers abound.

What do landscapers do in the winter?

The further north you go, the more seasonal it becomes of course. But if you live in say, Ohio, and fear that you'll only work three months of the year, relax. Ohio is a state where landscaping continues about nine to ten months of the year. Only in January and February, and in some years December, will it be difficult to find clients or install jobs.

To earn a living in northern states you need to either work longer hours during the season, charge more than your southern counterparts, or find a complimentary winter business such as snow removal. Most northern landscapers use all three strategies. The two to three slow or off months are used to line up work, maintain equipment, design new advertising, etc.

How difficult is this nut to crack?

One of the most attractive aspects of landscaping is that in most areas, the work is not difficult to find. A few thousand well-designed flyers printed up by your local printer and distributed door-to-door will almost surely bring in calls that will lead to jobs. Distribute a minimum of two thousand flyers and with a 1/4 to1/2% response rate (typical) you'll receive 50-100 calls. Turn 10% of those into jobs and you've lined up work that could last you much of the season.

Traditional advertising- flyers, space ads, classifieds in local papers, and yellow pages ads are all effective and can bring steady, predictable, results.

Many of the business opportunities in this book are highly competitive and the openings are limited in number, which can mean months or even years of trying, just to break into the field. Landscaping is competitive also, but there is so much work available, you can conceivably break in the very week you begin to advertise. This is one "creativity-required" business where the wheels turn quickly. And not just the wheels on your pickup truck either.

How can I tell if my landscape work is professional-level ?

Any of the following can be signs of a sub-par landscape installation:

☞ Large boulders accidentally installed *inside* a customer's house.

☞ Certain woeful looks accompanied by statements such as: "I wish you had told me I was at the wrong place *before* I cut down all the shrubs."

☞ You haven't seen the homeowner since you put the new driveway in and come to think of it, there's an awful big lump near the right corner.

Short of doing something extremely stupid, there is no right or wrong way to landscape a particular property. Because of that it's difficult to "evaluate" or grade a design. Different strokes for different folks and all that. If you don't take some sort of course or schooling you should consider working with an experienced landscaper before you strike out on your own.

Based on my experience...

Often, while my landscape business is in operation, I'm busy with other things (like music or writing or multiple landscape projects) and give a subordinate the design work on a particular job. Usually they approach it completely different from the way I would have and as a result, I'm skeptical of how it will be received by the client. Almost invariably, the client loves the design and once installed, we obtain many jobs from people who drive by, admire the work, and get our phone number from the homeowner or signs we place on jobsites.

* * *

If you have an artistic flair, and you follow a few basic design concepts such as: place smaller plants in front of larger ones; plant in groups of three, five, or more; trees generally look good on the corners; and upright shrubs like junipers or spruce frame a doorway nicely; then your basic design should turn out fine.

You must select individual plants according to things like their ability to take sun, tolerate drought and the type of soil they prefer.

Changes can easily be made to a landscape even after it is "finished" except for things like a permanent rock installation or cement work which might be difficult or expensive to modify. At first you can limit your projects to simple ones- jobs that require only plants and mulch and perhaps a lawn installation.

If this is a business you're serious about entering, learn the basics, then tackle that first project. There is no need to have your work evaluated by anyone.

Remember: if the homeowners don't like your design they always have the option of making changes or requesting a new design.

What monetary investment does this business require?

<u>Advertising</u>: You'll need at least $150 in advertising for enough fliers to get your business started. If you try other forms of advertising, you'll need far more money but you'll save time and energy spent delivering flyers.

<u>Hand Tools and Truck</u>: A good rake, shovel and wheelbarrow are essential and there are other tools you can buy as you go. Allow at least another $150 for these items.

A half-ton pickup truck is the vehicle the majority of landscapers start with. A 3/4 or one ton is an even better choice if you can afford one. Don't go overboard on the truck though. A dump is **not** an essential and will drain cash flow in slow months. You can have loads delivered and hauled at a reasonable cost. Most suppliers offer this service and it's absolutely the way to go when you're starting if money is tight.

Believe it or not, $300 to $600 plus whatever you pay for your truck and education (which could be from free books from the library) is all it takes to get started.

* * *

Put the author's experience to use:

It's better to keep equipment ownership on the back burner the first year, then if you decide to quit the business, it's a much easier decision. All the equipment you need to do a top-notch job can be obtained from a rental store. By renting, you don't drain cash flow with large payments that must be made during the months cash flow is poor. It may seem expensive and a bit of a hassle but there's hidden hassle and expense to owning equipment too.

I rented a front end loader and paid for the closest rental store to deliver it

One awesome machine

When it comes to moving dirt, preparing lawns for seeding, and almost any labor-intensive landscape task you can think of, there's almost certainly a machine that will do the job faster and better than the most muscle-laden human on earth.

Most rental companies will deliver a front-end loader like this one right to your jobsite. A loader usually pays for itself plus it's one heck of a lot easier on the labor- something to keep in mind if *you* are the labor.

to jobsites for the first five years I did landscaping. I finally did buy a new Bobcat loader *after* the business was established enough to support one.

* * *

You will need to study and do some research before you attempt to do a job. At minimum visit your local nursery to see what is for sale in your area, then take out some plant books from your local library and study the most common plant's shade, sun, and water needs plus other interesting characteristics. Prior to your first job you will also want to visit nurseries and landscape suppliers and discuss prices with them. Don't be afraid to ask for discounts. Suppliers and nurseries usually give you a break because you're buying in bulk.

It's a good idea to consider taking some type of training beyond just studying a book on plants. There are several formulas you should know to figure out things like: how many yards of mulch will be needed to cover 4,000 sq. feet? How many tons of topsoil will cover a certain area to a depth of 3 inches?, etc. So you'll have an investment in terms of time and money just for the learning phase. But there's big money in landscaping, so you'll likely quickly recoup anything you spend. And if you plan well, your investments in an education, truck and fliers will be the only ones you need to pay for upfront.....

* * *

Why pay for everything yourself? Why not let your first customer give you a helping hand? Here's the deal: you pay for the advertising, education, and truck and your first customer will buy you some hand tools to get you started.

The secret is that almost all large landscape jobs (over $300) pay half down. After banking the material money, there is usually cash left over, and you could use some of it to buy a few tools. Never, ever spend money earmarked for *materials* on anything else though, it's immoral and could get you in big trouble if you can't finish the job.

How much can you expect to make?

The *median* income for owners of landscape contracting businesses is $29,850. Over 65% report earning in excess of that figure. The author's landscape business was started part-time and as far as the time put into it, it still is. In spite of that, the business still built to a gross of some $84,000 by the fifth year.

How long will it take to see your first check?

From the day you begin distributing your flyers, you could have a down payment check in your hands within five days.

How long will it take to get established?

You should be able to support yourself almost immediately provided you start at the right time of year and diligently market your service.

You should be thoroughly established by the third year and an expert at running a landscape operation in 7-10 years.

Pricing

There are two main ways to price landscape jobs:

1. A flat rate per hour plus materials. Depending on your area and speed of your work, the going rate is normally between $25-$35 per man hour plus materials. You must calculate expected hours in advance and give an estimate.

2. A more time consuming but slightly more accurate method is to calculate each expense: actual labor cost per hour plus the

labor burden (workman's comp, taxes and insurance), plus materials, and calculate an estimate based on those figures.

If you are going to do the design work only, but no labor, start your service by consulting with each customer one time for free but charge a set amount to design and deliver drawings. A good starting point might be $75 for a complete plan plus photo costs. Any additional work could be billed at $40-60 per hour.

Is a computer necessary for design work?

No. If you're artistic, you can do very good designs without one. After you complete your first few jobs, pictures and drive-by references of previous jobs will help customers have confidence in your work.

Computer designs *can* save you time though, and will probably increase your sales ratio and improve your image. If you're focusing on design only, purchasing landscape software and a computer powerful enough to run it would be an excellent idea considering that will be your only major investment.

* * *

A Success Story

Back in 1988 I needed something to do with my free time. I was playing in bands about four or five nights a week, Wednesday through Sunday and the four-hour gigs were all within minutes of my house. With all my weekdays open I started looking for some type of business I could run at least three days a week.

My brothers had moved to Georgia and were making good money doing landscaping there. They had left home driving a beat-up van with the clothes on their back but returned for visits driving brand-new cars and wearing expensive threads. I figured if it worked for them, it would work for me.

I bought a used pickup truck and started running ads. Almost immediately I had filled my three day a week quota and continued expanding. Because I had my other commitments I expanded a lot slower than someone who did only landscaping would, still within a few years my little business had expanded enough to incorporate it.

In spite of the demands on my time I continue to landscape. Yes, I labor. The fresh air, exercise, and physical nature of the work provide a welcome contrast to the days I spend indoors pounding at a typewriter, polishing songs, programming drum machines, marketing my businesses, or other similar activities. Running a Bobcat is fun! Sometimes I run it on my own property just because it's so relaxing!

A Few (hundred) Words About Landscape Maintenance

Landscape maintenance is *not* what could be termed a "creativity-required" business. It includes everything that a person can do to keep a yard or landscape in good shape. Fertilizing, mowing lawns, pruning plants, and similar tasks all fit securely under the landscape maintenance umbrella. (And speaking of umbrella's- you might want to invest in one should you choose to go into the landscape field. Dealing with inclement weather is a certainty when you work outside much of the time.)

The reason maintenance is being mentioned in this book is because in some areas of the country if you don't offer maintenance, especially grass cutting, landscaping alone won't support you.

Cutting grass is a huge business in and of itself. A large percentage of the 12 billion dollars landscapers take in annually in the U.S. can be attributed purely to mowing. If you enter the landscape field it will be hard not to notice rival landscape firm's trucks loaded to the brim with commercial walk-behind mowers and fertilizing equipment.

There are several points that should be noted:

☞ You don't *have* to do maintenance to run a successful landscape operation in most areas.

☞   The reason most landscape firms do maintenance is to maintain a steadier cash flow. They see landscaping as their "big money" and cutting as their cash flow.

☞   If you intend to run this business alone, it would be best to choose either landscaping or maintenance. You could do both but since you can't run two separate dedicated crews, focusing on one activity will automatically drive profits up.

☞   Just because landscaping is the more glamorous of the two activities does not mean there can't be good money in both. Using modern equipment can push mowing up into the $40 per man hour range.

☞   Landscaping requires a steady flow of one-time jobs and that means constant bidding. Mowing or fertilizing jobs are repeat jobs. Once you set a mowing list, you don't need to do bids except to replace customers you lose.

There's grow up and branch out potential

There are many landscape firms that start as one-man operations and grow. And grow. And grow. Landscape magazines are full of profiles of companies from throughout the U.S. who gross from one half million to over ten million dollars annually.

In summary

Designing landscapes from scratch is akin to taking a blank palette and painting in 3-D to create a living piece of art. Few things in life will give you as much self-satisfaction (or as much exercise) as taking a plain property and turning it into something that looks like a picture on a postcard.

A Walk-Behind Mower

Walk-behind commercial mowers are powerful high-speed cutting machines. Price range? $2,500 to over $5,000 per unit but they can make mowing quick and profitable.

And landscaping is a business with other advantages. Even the installation part requires some degree of creativity, plus you get to work outdoors. And once you start doing landscaping labor regularly, you can let your Bally's membership expire, that's for sure. But of course it's not for everyone.

It does require some degree of physical endurance and no matter what machinery you have, there are times when physical strength is required. Still, anyone who enjoys being outside a lot and would like to get paid to stay in shape should give serious thought to the potential career landscaping offers.

For Further Study:

Learning the Landscape and Lawn Maintenance Business. This is an easy-to-read-and-follow course designed for the student who wants to save money (about 1/3 to 1/2 the cost of other mail order courses), wants to learn fast, and doesn't require a lot of hand-holding (there is no tedious mailing back and forth, just one test upon completion of the course). Based on the techniques used successfully by Pro Lawn Industries, Inc. $225 postage paid gets the entire course shipped to your doorstep in one package. Creative Books, P. O. Box 463, Beaver, PA 15009-0463.

Reader's Digest's *Illustrated Guide to Gardening.* A comprehensive guide to shrubs, plants, and trees. Reader's Digest Books. This is a "must have". You'll find this text indispensable. ISBN: 0-89577-046-6.

Step-By-Step Landscaping. This book covers plants but far less extensively than the Reader's Digest book. The real value of having this volume is the wealth of information it contains on lawns, grading, hardscaping, etc. Rodale Books.

Sensible Software. 301-874-3611. Their software program "Clip" is one of the best programs for lawn <u>maintenance</u> (grass cutting) job tracking available. If your business grows rapidly you may find the high price tag (approx. $700 for the smallest 125 customer version) well worth the price considering its capabilities.

Home Guide to Lawns and Landscaping. The title should be self-explanatory. You can find this through the publisher, Harper & Rowe but there are probably other very adequate books available on this subject in your local library.

Greenline. 1-800-356-0171. This mail order company publishes a catalog of landscaper's tools and parts.

ALCA. 1-800-395-2522. This is one of the best known landscaper's associations. Call or visit their website at http://www.alca.org.

Landscape Designer. and similar homeowner grade software programs allow you to take a photo of a jobsite, scan it into a computer, add realistic looking plants and other images, and then print the results. They are available from various mail order computer software catalogs or your local computer store can order them. A more professional (and costly) design program is *Landsuite Professional 1-800-480-0222*. Programs on this level can design, total up the materials automatically as you add the images, and bill the customer.

Chapter Seven

Recording Studio and Demo Work

The lights are what you notice first. It seems like they're everywhere. Tiny amber specks that signify the amps are on and ready to blast out some bass or guitar if needed. The cassette decks keep flashing red and the drum machine's little green dot is pulsating right in time to the music. A small ray of white shines from each vu meter.

Then you see the knobs. Gadjillions of them. The mixer looks like something from *Star Wars* and you're thinking "I better not touch those things. If I turn the wrong one, I'll either ruin the whole session or put us on a trajectory to Jupiter".

Your eyes finally land on a man sitting at the board. He's actually touching the knobs. He listens, he tweaks a fader, listens some more, and pushes a button.... "The dude knows what he's doing," you think.

And for a few seconds you wish you were him...

Thousands of people in the United States make their living from owning and operating recording studios. There are project studios, demo services, and full-service facilities. Some of these studios focus mainly on recording music, while others record everything from the audio portion of videotapes and films, to audio books for people with vision problems. Some studios record sports fantasy tapes or self-help cassettes, while others focus on commercial advertising work.

What's it really like?

Recording is a blast. Even recording other people's stuff is a blast. Even recording the sound of a dog barking into a microphone through a harmonizer, a phase shifter, a reverb unit, and a sonic maximizer is a blast. So owning a recording service is one blast after another, right?

Right. But in between those blasts, there's a lot of work to be done. Work like storing and cataloging tapes, keeping the books, marketing, and selling the studio to prospective clients.

If all that doesn't scare you off, then let's take an in-depth look at this business to see if it really is right for you.

What is recording?

Recording, the way we use it in this book, means to capture audio material in a permanent and retrievable form on magnetic tape or digitally.

Why does a market exist for recording services?

Obviously, once a sound is created by a sound source, be it a tuba, a crowd, a speaker, or whatever, it may never be repeated in quite the same way again. People want to capture some of those sounds. They want to be able to listen to them repeatedly, in a convenient form, whenever they wish.

Consumers want to listen to music in their car, for example, without setting up a whole band in the back seat. They want to learn from a famous doctor they see on TV, but don't want to pay him to visit them personally. They will, however, pay $13.99 for the cassette "10 Tips to End Your Constipation Problems Forever".

When people listen to these sounds, they want them to be clear, not muffled. They want them to sound as close as possible to the real thing, or even better than the original, if possible.

To achieve the high quality recordings demanded by consumers requires top-of-the-line recording equipment operated by knowledgeable professionals. Even if you can get a clear recording from a consumer-grade deck, later copies will degrade noticeably from the original. And the consumer market is huge, demanding a lot of copies. So the need exists for studios that can record these sounds on such high quality equipment, that there is little or no degradation of the sound on the product the consumer purchases.

Where is the work?

There is work for recording engineers throughout the country but it is definitely a tight market. Recording schools produce many qualified engineers each year who may never find steady work. A more sure path to being employed in this business is to startup your own studio.

Most big cities have several successful recording facilities and there are established studios in certain smaller towns throughout most geographic areas. You can check your local yellow pages under "Recording" and "Recording Studios". The lack of a facility in your area could indicate a need exists or it could indicate that there is no market for this service in your local area.

Small town studios were once strictly full-service and usually *had to* do a wide variety of things to survive, but there is now a trend toward highly-focused project studios.

There is a huge volume of music recording, and recording in general, being done in Nashville, New York, and Los Angeles, but that doesn't necessarily mean you must or even should relocate to one of these music meccas. It might be a good move for you because more work is there, but you need to realize: the huge amount of competition in those cities drives down the price. Sometimes to unprofitable levels. You might charge a very reasonable $60/hour for your studio time and get it in Ohio; in L. A. you may get $25/hour for the same equipment.

There is one other route you can take, although it is a difficult and expensive one- a mail order recording service that can be run from anywhere. It's doubly difficult because you are starting and learning two separate businesses- recording and mail order- simultaneously. The mail order possibilities range from recording and selling tapes and CDs of your own design (beware, now you're adding a third business, self-publishing!), to recording professional versions of other's scripts, songs, and similar things by mail.

Is it hard to succeed in this business?

Recording services open often and close almost as often. The main reasons for failure are:

1. Lack of knowledge about business in general.

2. Failure to purchase professional-level equipment.

81

Artist-produced CD's and tapes

It's harder than ever to get signed to a major-label contract these days....inspiring many people to "roll their own" product, often with considerable success. The Internet and advancing low-cost, high-quality recording technology are helping to fuel the movement toward self-production.

3. Lack of consistent marketing efforts.

4. Incorrect pricing (too low is most common).

5. Failure to research and test adequately to see if there is a need for the service in the area.

6. Failure to understand the recording business.

That last point accounts for as many failures as all the other reasons combined because opening a studio is such a natural progression for a musician. And musicians, naturally enough, associate recording with music.

We'll let Chuck, a musician who's worked with countless local bands tell his story to illustrate the point:

A Non-Success Story

"I was tired of one night stands five or six nights a week so I opened *Chuck's Recording* in 1996, using three rooms of my downstairs. I soundproofed everything in the main recording room, put a window between it and the control room, and had a little office area/entranceway- a real nice setup. I even had separate booths for vocals and drums. Then I ran ads in the local papers to let musicians know I was open for business, and really, really pushed it to every musician I knew. People recorded here and some came back again, but I never could keep the place booked full time. I decided it wasn't worth it and closed up after trying it for about two years."

Chuck's Recording didn't make it, at least in part, because Chuck did not understand the business. Being a musician the word recording meant one thing to him: recording music. Every time he had been in a studio, he was there recording music. The owner or manager of the studio always mentioned names of other local bands that had been in lately, the walls of the place were covered with records musicians had made there....So Chuck *assumed* that studios made most of their money from musicians. In reality, being in a very small market, the successful studios enjoyed recording musicians and pushed that aspect of it; however, the bulk of their gross revenues resulted from commercial work. Local commercial advertising spots for radio and TV, documentary soundtracks, and similar things accounted for most of the dollars they made, not musicians recording songs.

Chuck designed his studio and paid for advertising that targeted a market that could never have supported his operation. Know what your real business is before you start it!

This is not an easy business to succeed in but certainly not an impossible one. A recording service requires more of an investment than most other businesses in this book so you must learn all you can about both the recording business and business in general before you start. A course in small business management would be an excellent start.

What financial investment is required?

It depends on what type of studio you feel you can open successfully and what type of clients you will serve.

First you must determine if a single-purpose project studio would work in your area. That would be the easiest and least costly type of facility to setup.

The higher the concentration of people in the area of the studio, the more you can focus on one particular type of client, and the less investment is necessary. Especially if the niche you choose is one that's untapped by the competition. For the purposes of this book we'll look more in-depth at two possibilities- the cheapest possible type of studio, and an entry-level full service facility. First, a little background information on multi-track is in order.

* * *

A Multi-track Primer

When you record sounds on a simple home cassette deck, you record in stereo. To achieve stereo, the cassette tape you record on is divided into four sections running the entire length of the tape. The first section is for the left part of the signal and the adjacent section is for the right part.

The two remaining sections do the same thing but only if you flip the tape over to play the other side. In a sense you could say a regular old cassette tape has 4 tracks- Side "A" left and right are two tracks, and Side "B" left and right are the other two.

Now if you used those same four sections of the cassette tape but recorded them all at the same time while the tape moved in only one direction, you would be recording all 4 tracks at once.

If those four tracks were separated- free to accept any signal from any source, rather than just the left and right part of a given program- you would be recording multiple independent tracks, also known as "multi-tracking". Here's how it works:

Multi-track recorders make it possible to record the drums, back the tape up, then listen to the drums while the bass player records the bass on a separate track. Now you can play those two tracks back together to listen to the blend of the music. If one is too loud you can adjust the volume level of either the bass or the drums with a knob dedicated to that purpose called a fader. You can continue to back up the tape adding instruments to the piece with each pass until all the available tracks are filled up.

Once you have recorded all the parts you wish to record, you then listen to all the tracks back at once, adjusting each track's fader until the blend or "mix" is just right. Multi-track recorders are the heart of a recording studio and the more "tracks" or passes the machine is built to accept, the more expensive the machine becomes. The most common number of tracks on a multi-track machine are 4, 8, 16, or 24.

The Toyota

The simplest type of studio to set up would be geared to individual songwriters or duos and trios using acoustic instruments. It would be a single-purpose studio- for demo tapes only. You wouldn't need a lot of renovation to your facility or even multiple rooms. Because there would only be perhaps one or two instruments and a few harmonies, an 8 track unit would work fine. Since it's a demo facility, and dedicated to musicians only, you wouldn't need to invest in expensive audio-to-video sync lock devices or anything beyond the most basic recording gear.

A couple mics, a mixing board, a decent quality digital 8 track unit and accessories might set you back $7,000-$12,000. You can expect the equipment to last at least 5 years so pro-rated that's $1,400 to $2,400 per year.

Nashville comes to mind as a place this type of setup might flourish. The right advertising to snag new songwriters just after they hop off the bus would supply a steady stream of new clients. Quality work would bring them back.

The Cadillac

A full blown multi-purpose 24 track (or more) studio would necessitate at least some renovation and true professional-level equipment. Considering that one mic could cost two thousand dollars, a decent multitrack unit $20,000 or more, renovation another $20,000 to $50,000 well... you know the old saying: $20,000 here, $50,000 there, pretty soon it adds up to big money. When you figure in the fact that you need extensive arrays of signal processors and audio-video capabilities you could be looking at $100,000 or more just for an entry-level facility. Many established studios have equipment approaching a half a million dollars in cost. Of course the rates they command are correspondingly high.

Somewhere between these two setups are a multitude of investment levels. But you can't put the cart before the horse, if research is telling you that a certain type of facility will not work in your area, you can't go ahead with the idea just because that's all you can afford and "your heart's set on having a studio". Secure additional funding or move to an area where the facility you *can* afford will work.

How much can you expect to make?

Downtime really kills you in the studio business. Your expenses are nearly identical whether the equipment is in use or not. Managed properly, the owner of a full blown successful studio can expect to net $50-80 thousand dollars a year while a small project studio owner can expect to see $18-25 thousand if he keeps overhead low and bookings solid.

How long before I see my first check?

Assuming your planning and renovation is complete, from the day you hang out your shingle, until you have a check in hand, figure at least two weeks to a month. That's how long it would take to get your first call, show the studio to the client, schedule a date and complete a medium size project.

If you go the mail-order route, figure anywhere from two to three months because magazines, which is where you're most likely to find your target audience, generally work at least one to two full months ahead (plus a few days are lost as mail travels back and forth between the client and the studio). Some magazines need ad copy up to six months in advance.

If you can't wait eight months to get paid you can eliminate this waiting period by submitting your ads before you open your business so they are timed to appear when you need them to.

How long will it take to get established?

Getting past the second year is the hardest period. In this business, if you can hold on for five years, you are established and may even be top dog by virtue of being the only studio around. Recording is like poker though. The basics are easy to learn but the subtleties can take a lifetime. And technology keeps improving making it difficult to stay up-to-date.

Pricing Your Service

Competition, quality of your equipment and location dramatically affect the rate you can charge, but almost invariably studio time is billed according to an hourly rate. Sometimes blocks of time are sold in advance at a discount. For example you might charge $70 per hour for a 16 track facility but if the client is willing to purchase an 8 hour block of time and pay in advance, perhaps the price drops to $450. Recording tape is almost always extra since one client may use 3 minutes of master tape in a given time while someone else may use two times as much. With digital recording there is no tape; everything is saved digitally, so you charge for the disks or DATs or whatever storage medium is used.

Most twenty four track facilities charge in the $100/hr. and up range, 16 track facilities get $40-80/hr. and 8 track drops off to around $25/hr. but these rates are just a guideline. It's essential that you set up a budget and figure out what you need to charge to stay in business. Checking competitors rates is risky since there may only be a few facilities and they may be undercharging, or have vastly inferior equipment to yours.

Ideas for marketing your studio

Business cards- the old standby- are effective. But don't expect much, if any, immediate business. Future customers will accept your card but might carry it in a wallet or hang it on a wall for a while (maybe even years) before they need your service. Some cards will be thrown away but if the potential client believes your service might be useful someday, it will be retained.

The potential for business cards to 1. Let people know you're in business at all 2. Generate third-party referrals as in "Hey Joe, know of any good studios?" and 3. To bring in business when you least expect it, is enormous. Cards are inexpensive- get them in circulation as soon as possible. Don't waste them but "if in doubt, hand it out" is a good rule.

Hang them up at music stores, give them out with every mailing. It's funny how many businesses go out of business in less than one year with boxes of unused business cards that are thrown away.

A lot of prospective clients will use the Yellow Pages to find a studio. If you are not "in the book", you will lose business.

A free newsletter, mailed to anyone who inquires about your business or uses your service is an excellent idea for a studio. It inexpensively lets you position yourself as an expert, keep your studio name in everyone's face, advertise special prices on blocks of time at off-peak times and spark a client's interest in getting into the studio again.

Occasional space ads in local, general interest newspapers and trade journals (local musician's magazines for example) are effective at pulling in a few people who wouldn't find you through other sources. Don't run them too often or you could eat up a lot of money targeting only a few potential customers. Twice a year would be plenty in a local newspaper.

It's worth repeating: word-of-mouth is your best advertising. Traditional advertising acts as the catalyst for the word-of-mouth process.

The author's experience

My own studio, Play It Again Demos, principally caters to songwriters and publishers. We run classified and space ads in various print mediums to locate clients, then use a two-step ad (see the self-publishing chapter "How Much Money You Can Make" section for an explanation of two-step ads) to attempt to secure an order.

It took about 4 to 5 years before I really felt like the business was established, and still we occasionally experience extended periods of time without much work.

Often we get second orders from clients we first worked for many years prior, which is part of the reason it takes so long to get established. As I write this, in fact, we just completed a three song project for a client from Canada who we last worked for well over two years ago and hadn't heard from until recently. Another recent project came in from a client we hadn't heard from in over five years.

On the other hand, we do have a couple of customers who've given us work pretty regularly since the service started back in the early '90's.

One huge drawback about this business for me at first was: once I began running a studio for pay, my own songwriting- the stuff I wrote and recorded both for my own pleasure and for my own songwriting career suffered. Maybe not in quality, but in quantity. It seemed like there was always one more thing that should be done for Play It Again- like marketing the studio, or a mix, or pre-production work. If I took time out for my own material, I felt I was robbing time from the business. That problem mostly solved itself once the business generated enough work to hire a few other people. As I write this in fact, I'm doing more writing and co-writing than I've ever done before.

All in all, a demo studio is a nice little operation to own. On occasion I sit down in the producer's seat and turn down the lights so I can see the tiny instrument panel lights glowing in various hues of yellow, red, and green. I sit there skillfully pushing faders as I listen intently to the mix. Occasionally I tweak one of the gadzillion knobs, and for a few moments instead of thinking "I wish I were the man in that chair," I *am* the man in the chair.

A Human Voice Synthesizer

Technology has permanently changed the amount of work available for human musicians- including singers. The device pictured above can change a male voice to female, generate up to six accurate harmony parts, and can help you do one darn fantastic imitation of Popeye.

Fiddle with these buttons and knobs a while. If you can't create a great song production, maybe you can be the first person to land on Venus.

Other advantages and disadvantages

One big plus to owning a studio is that it can provide you with connections to other people in the music industry. Just about any studio that establishes itself as "the" place to cut a CD or demo tape will record its share of hit songs and have celebrities stop in to record projects they need to complete while they are on the road.

Also, you can gain a lot of producing and mixing experience, plus if you do have energy left over to do your own projects you'll have quality equipment to work on and complete control over it.

Now for a few of the bad things. First of all, most of the businesses in this book are fairly easy to move to a new location. A recording studio is not so easy to relocate. It can be done of course but the business can hardly be described as portable. Second, most businesses in this book don't tie you down to a certain location to actually perform the work. Even writing, which seems like it would tie you to a desk, allows you to occasionally grab a notebook computer and go to a local park to work. Studios don't permit you that option. You're stuck in the studio, or get the privilege of being there, (depending on how you view it) 8-12 hours a day.

Third, to be a home-based studio, you are required to give up a substantial portion of your home immediately. Other businesses may grow to slowly engulf several rooms, but recording requires that sacrifice right up front.

Starting a studio is a huge undertaking. And once you've invested money and time in building one, you will be investing a great deal more time and money making it a success. Be sure you think through everything thoroughly before committing one cent to actual construction.

For Further Study:

The following title is available from Creative Books:

Hot Tips For The Home Recording Studio. by Hank Linderman. A wealth of home recording advice for musicians and beginning producers. $21.50

Orders for the above title should be sent to:

Creative Books
P. O. Box 463
Beaver, PA 15009-0463

Check or money order only. Money orders are faster. PA residents must add 6% sales tax. Price includes shipping and handling and the most recent edition in print will be shipped. Should a price increase occur, you will be notified (or send extra and the overpayment will be refunded).

How to Run a Recording Session by Jayce De Santis. The title is self-explanatory and the book is available at major bookstores like Barnes and Noble or from Soundstream P.O. Box 640163, Oakland Gardens, NY 11364-0163. It's $9.95 but you should inquire about shipping charges before ordering.

Musician's Friend P.O.B. 4520, Medford, OR 97501 has several books and videos which will help solidify your knowledge of the basic recording process including:

The Musician's Guide to Home Recording a book which details how to make professional recordings at home.

Basic Multitrack Recording Tips. If you have to ask what this is about perhaps you need to re-read the title. It's goal is to help you achieve top quality recordings with a minimum of learning time.

Musician's Friend also carries a full line of recording equipment by makers such as Lexicon, Roland, Eventide, Fostex, Teac and many more. The majority of the recording gear is semi-pro, not commercial grade professional, but some of it is pro, mainly the microphones and some of the signal processing equipment.

For better grade mulititrack machines try Sam Ash Music Stores. Their catalog is available by writing to P.O. Box 9047 Hicksville, NY 11802.

Your local music store (ask musician's for the location of the biggest one in your area) may have a great deal of equipment information you'll find helpful. Be sure to tell the salesman what your intention is- to build a pro commercial studio. Don't let him sell you the most expensive semi-pro gear he has in stock.

Studio Sound is a monthly magazine that covers pro audio worldwide. Contact Miller Freeman Entertainment Ltd., 8 Montague Close, London Bridge, London SE1 9UR.

Recording is also a monthly. A little less technical than *Studio Sound* but not so pro-oriented. 1-303-516-9118.

Mix P.O. Box 41525, Nashville, TN 37204-9830. The magazine for the working studio pro.

NRS 1-800-538-2336 has blank cassette tape, recordable CD's, and DAT tapes that you can purchase in quantity.

In the November 2000 issue of Mix magazine, Tom Misner, owner of the SAE chain of recording schools (he currently owns 30 facilities throughout the world) says this about entering the recording business: "You have to know how to work with people, not just machines. Some people know everything but fail, because they have no communication skills." That's true for most businesses. Still, if you intend to own and operate a recording business, you must know how to use the equipment. Here are just a few of the dozens of schools throughout the U.S. that offer courses in audio recording. They offer everything from simple, informal seminars to master and bachelor degrees in audio recording:

Recording Connection; Hollywood, CA 1-800-295-4433.

Woodland Studios; Nashville, TN 615-262-2222.

Institute of Audio Research; NY, NY 212-777-8550.

MTSU; Murfreesboro, TN 615-898-5682.

Synergetic Audio; Greenville, IN 812-923-3610.

Omega Recording School; Rockville, MD 301-230-9100.

Chapter Eight

Plant Growing

Why is plant growing included in a book about creativity-required businesses? It's simple: when the growing isn't going well, it requires creativity and experimentation to figure out effective solutions. And talent is absolutely a requirement in certain aspects of selling plants you grow- from making attractive flower arrangements, to decorating plant pots, to pruning ornamentals into shapes that increase their value- the list is a long one.

There are two main markets you can grow for- the commercial market or the consumer market. The commercial market would encompass growing for nurseries, landscapers, supermarkets or any other business which re-sells the plants. Growing for the consumer market of course, means to grow for, and sell directly to, the individual buyer.

What is Plant Growing?

Plant growing entails either starting your chosen product from seed and growing on to a sellable size or purchasing seedlings and then selling them when they reach the size needed by the market. During that process you must choose soil mixes, fertilizers and watering times that are optimum for each plant. In most growing operations you will be required to transplant, prune and apply insect and disease controls as necessary. You must ensure that temperatures and sunlight amounts are ideal for the plant. In some operations you must prepare plants for shipping and make them look attractive as possible for the consumer.

Why Does a Market Exist for Plants?

Although on the surface it appears that a person purchases a tomato seedling because it provides food, tomatoes can be purchased at a store quite cheaply with far less effort and time expended than would be required to grow one.

So why do so many people grow tomatoes? Often it's just because they enjoy growing things, or because getting out in the back yard is relaxing or because growing tomatoes brings back memories of the family garden. And in rare cases it's because they need ammunition to throw at neighbors they don't like- all reasons that have nothing to do with the actual food value.

Most people enjoy the beauty and comfort some plants provide. All types of people. For many of them it would be unthinkable not to have at least a few plants around their house, and inside it too. For other people, having plants is an obsession. And plants don't last forever. They become old and unattractive. Some are mistreated and die prematurely. Some plants are annuals, lasting only a year. As these plants are replaced, it creates a steady market for new plants.

Where are the opportunities?

Plants can be grown successfully in almost every area of the United States. The opportunities to sell them locally abound. Flea markets, farmer's markets, plant auctions, garden centers, roadside stands, nurseries, wholesaling to landscapers and floral shops are just some of the places you might sell to.

In addition, almost every type of annual, perennial, tree, shrub, or vegetable plant is sold successfully by mail order. But mail order isn't always the answer. It's expensive to start a mail order operation and people in other areas may not want the types of plants you are able to grow.

Relocation may be necessary if you live in an exceptionally poor growing location or there's very few people around to sell to. Relocation may also be necessary simply to compete. If you wish to grow a certain type of plant but can do so only in a greenhouse, southern growers may kill your business with lower prices.

Thorough research is an absolute must before starting a plant growing business. Plants can be grown in most locations throughout the U.S. but just because someone near you is successfully growing and selling junipers doesn't mean you will be able to duplicate that success. Perhaps that grower has a deal with a local nursery to sell them so many plants wholesale each year, and maybe that's all the plants that nursery needs. Or another example: you wouldn't want to spend 5 years growing hundreds of sugar maple trees just because it's something you found you can grow successfully, then find out nurseries don't want any sugar maples but they'll take every Japanese maple they can get their hands on.

You're going to have to get out and observe places where plants are sold. Talk to the owners of garden centers and other places who might be interested in buying wholesale from you. Ask them what they need and would be willing to buy from you if you grow it (if their hair is kind of long, their eyes look a little funny and they offer to share their pipe with you after you ask that question, find another garden center). Beware- a certain plant may be in short supply for a couple years and due to the law of supply and demand the price increases. Growers will respond by increasing production and two years later the bottom can fall out of the market. Try to grow something that is fairly common and has a steady demand- tomato plants or azaleas or spruce trees for example.

If you're growing for the consumer market figure out where sales are occurring and when. Try to ascertain how much product can be moved at a particular location. For example....

* * *

A Success Story, Sales Gimmick and Research Technique Rolled Into One

Every Friday there's a flea market in Rogers, Ohio. It's one of the biggest in the country. From early spring until late fall three or four competing growers rent spaces there. All four sell one thing: ornamental shrubs in one gallon pots. Because I've (the author) seen those same growers there for several years I know they're making money, otherwise they would not waste their time. I've bought plants from them several times and heard them mention things like "slow day today" or "this is the first day I've sold out this early." I've observed other people purchasing plants there.

The plants are priced only slightly less than retail but since most ornamentals are sold in two gallon pots at other locations, not one gallons, they seem like a steal- an important point since the vendors are selling to "flea market mentality" bargain hunters. The growers setup their plants in rows about twenty deep with about 15 rows across. Every row or two features a different variety. The average price is $5 to $10 per plant so if they sell out, which they often do, they must gross $1,500-3,000 dollars for a day.

I've never sold plants there but if I were going to I'd try to figure out 1. How many plants a grower would move in a season: (stop early in the day to count plants and late to see how many sold). Do this several times throughout the season. 2. Determine if they have additional sales outlets by asking them for a variety of plant they don't have with them that they did have last time. When they say "I can have one next week" ask if there's another market they'll be at between now and then so you can pick it up sooner (do stop to get it). 3. Look into renting a spot. Some great locations may be reserved for years in advance, maybe no spots are even available unless someone gives one up. 4. If a site can be had, jump in and give it a try. Purchase some similar product wholesale, in this instance some one-gallon ornamentals, and sell them. This would give you a chance to see if you enjoy this type of selling. Better to spend a few hundred dollars now than invest years in growing product only to find out you don't like it. Yes, you might get stuck with ornamentals you can't move but if you can't move these ones, how could you possibly move fifty or a hundred times that amount? If you want to sell at this type of market just do it and think positive: If you do move these experimental plants, you'll make a nice profit.

* * *

Your research must find a plant or plants that you

☞ Are capable of growing successfully

☞ Have the room to grow

☞ Can grow fast enough to suit your needs

☞ Are able to find sales outlets for

The third point is important. Trees and shrubs can take years to grow to a sellable size while annuals take only weeks. Do you need cash fast or is this just a secondary income?

Can Your Plants Compete In Terms of Quality?

We've all seen Christmas trees Dad brought home after he had one too many at the Christmas party the night before. The tree looked like it had been dragged home tied *behind* the car instead of tied on the roof. The kind of tree Charlie Brown would be proud of. The kind of tree *no one* else would select unless their head was pounding so severely that they couldn't concentrate on anything, let alone on buying a tree that actually had needles.

If many of the plants you grow have that Charlie Brown look, well, you've got problems. People buy full, lush, healthy-looking plants. Anything less and they keep their money in their wallet. So how do you know if you're measuring up to people's expectations before you take your plants to market?

You must occasionally purchase a healthy specimen of about the same age as yours and compare. If you're growing trees to sell in five years, at one year buy a one year seedling from a reputable grower and see how your trees compare in terms of color, vigor, branching, fullness, height and spread. Do this at least once a year. If you see a problem area, immediately seek advice from a horticulturist. Try to prevent problems in the first place by using the correct soil mixtures, quality seed or seedlings, fertilizers, watering procedures, etc. Always follow instructions to the letter. Remember- it's unlikely a plant expert would take the trouble to say "Thoroughly water every five days," if a cupful of water every five days is sufficient. Chances are without thorough watering in sufficient quantities, the root system of the plant in question will show weak development.

Anytime you ignore specific advice you can expect problems to surface that could have been prevented.

When your plants are nearing sale size and measure up to your test plants in every respect, you can put them on the market in full confidence that they are the equal of any other grower's product.

How much space is required?

To judge the amount of growing space required, you will have to determine the amount of income you must make from your plant business; how much profit you can expect to earn per plant; how many separate crops you will need to grow to ensure a harvest year after year (a steady yearly supply of trees that will be culled at 7 years of age means that during the seventh year, seven crops each the size of a one-year supply must be grown simultaneously); how many extra plants you'll plant to allow for disease, winterkill and other problems that will diminish your output; and a rough estimate of how much room each plant needs at each stage of growth. Some useful facts:

☞ Most plants should be started in small containers and moved up as they grow in order to conserve space and avoid root problems.

☞ Perennials and annuals can be started directly in four-inch-square pots. They may sell before they must be transplanted.

☞ Most shrubs and trees do not need to be field grown. Many growers now grow shrubs in pots, which conserves a great deal of space in the field. Simply bury the pots in the ground to winter them over.

☞ A one gallon pot is a little over 6 inches across. A two gallon pot- the most common size shrubs are sold at- is about 9 inches. Some room left between shrubs is advisable in order to avoid bare spaces on foliage where plants touch.

☞ Allow for walking space to tend the crops.

☞ Purchase or borrow a book on the specific plant varieties you intend to grow to determine precise needs for space.

Focus On Business Basics

If you focus on the major success strategies that can make any business succeed, the details tend to fall into place.

• There must be a demand for your product or service.

• Your pricing must be in line with what customers are willing to pay, but underpricing leads to lack of profit and possibly business failure.

• Cash flow is the lifeblood of business. Good invoicing and accounts receivable collections are mandatory.

• An all-encompassing marketing program is essential (see pgs. 15-18). Include stellar customer service and what business guru, Dr. W. Edward Deming, calls *delight factors*- unexpected free extras that increase a customer's satisfaction with the buying process. (Deming originated the "continual improvement forever" concept that permitted Japan to dominate world business in the1980s).

What monetary investment is required?

The amount of start-up money needed can vary substantially. To grow 1,000 flats of annual flowers from seed in Florida is far less costly than growing 1,000 flats of spring annuals in Maine where a greenhouse and heating it is part of the investment. Yet growing *shrubs* from seedlings in the north does *not* require a greenhouse (in fact, shrubs must go dormant in winter or they will die) keeping start-up costs at a reasonable level.

You must figure out what conditions are required for you to grow your particular plant or plants in your particular area. Here are a few guidelines:

1. The most expensive components to growing plants (other than labor) are land and greenhouses. A greenhouse can cost anywhere from several hundred dollars for a small homeowner non-commercial model (though they *are* used by some people to grow plants for money) up to tens of thousands of dollars for a full-blown commercial model.

2. Most annuals and vegetables can be started from seed cheaply as most seed packets are under $2 and contain hundreds of seeds. In the north; however, you'll likely need a greenhouse (or an awful lot of windows in your home) to grow annuals or vegetable starter plants for market. You must figure in the cost of the flats (trays that will start 50-500 seedlings) required also. A case of 100 trays is about $60. Don't forget water and fertilizer costs which would probably be under $100 for the season. 3 cubic feet of a soilless mix is about $10 which fills about 150 4-inch pots (the 4 inch pots are what you'll transplant

the seedlings to eventually and possibly sell them in). 1,000 4-inch pots cost about $35. For under $1,500 you can grow 10,000 plants. The greenhouse installation and maintenance costs would be added to that total if one is necessary.

3. Perennials (plants that die off in winter but then come back each spring) can be started from seed. The seeds come in packs that costs under $2 but some varieties may only have a few seeds per pack while others may have hundreds. For many varieties, starting from seed is just as inexpensive as annuals, but perennials take longer to get established, thus commanding a higher price. Many perennials are also easily and inexpensively started from cuttings and divisions of "mother" plants. Most perennials winter over in the ground with no additional protection.

4. Trees and shrubs. You'll probably want to start trees and shrubs from seedlings purchased from other nurseries. Most seedlings are under $2 per plant and can be as low as 50 cents with additional price breaks for large quantities. The stock can normally be wintered-over outside if the pots are buried in earth but sometimes require burlap barriers or other protection. No greenhouse is necessary. To grow 1,000 trees that will eventually sell for $50 each you may only need to invest $500-$2,000 upfront each year. (Plus the cost of the land you're growing on for as many years as it takes for the trees to mature). You can't just plant them and forget them though. Pruning and fertilizing will be required periodically. If you're growing trees or shrubs in pots, they'll require a great deal of watering during hot, dry periods. Disease and insects can become problematic and will require prompt attention.

As you can see from the preceding estimates, growing plants does not require a huge investment upfront for supplies. It's the space and greenhouse that can be expensive. You can start much smaller than in the examples and expand as you gain confidence in your ability to successfully grow plants.

Advertising

The greatest plants in the world won't sell if no one knows where to find them. It recommended that you research sales methods that are working for other growers, then develop at least a one-year advertising plan to determine an ad budget. For local selling, an ad in the yellow pages supplemented with flyers and occasional newspaper ads is a good place to start, but by carefully researching the local market you may add to those basic methods or eliminate some of them as unpractical for your area. Many growers do well selling only at flea markets or roadside stands.

* * *

The First Year is the Hardest

Sherry Palmer, a grower in Chehalis, a town in Washington state, enjoyed gardening and garden design for many years as a hobby before launching her own business, Creekside Gardens, less than one year ago.

Her sister, the owner of Herban Renewal Nursery and Herb Garden in Seattle, provided the original stock for Creekside, along with plenty of business advice and horticultural experience.

Currently producing perennials, herbs, and woody ornamentals, she plans to choose a specialty soon, then concentrate on growing that one thing. According to Sherry, " It is very easy to get fragmented by trying to grow too many species each with their special requirements. To be commercially viable, it is necessary to specialize so your production, marketing and sales efforts can be concentrated."

She feels that growing plants is an excellent career and that the demand for plants is increasing. Most of her sales are through a local farmer's market but she's also experimenting with wholesale, retail and even e-commerce.

Sherry's advice to those thinking of entering the business? "You need some kind of financial support for at least the first couple of years until the business becomes established and can support you. For many people that means a full-time job in addition to running the business."

* * *

How to set prices

You can attempt to figure up all your costs involved in the production of a certain plant, add in what you want to make per hour, add a 30 per cent labor burden (for workman's comp, insurance, etc.) and add your expected profit to determine a price. This is a tedious method but many growers use it because if figured accurately, it helps determine what you must charge to stay in business based on your particular costs. A system is only as good as the numbers entered into it however, and it's difficult to believe that a person could accurately determine exactly how much of a water bill should be attributed to the petunias and how much to the marigolds.

An easier way is to set a price by visiting 5 or 6 competitors, toss out the low and high price, average the rest, and start selling at the average price for that particular plant. It's not the method recommended by most business management manuals but it will establish a reasonable starting point. Later through profit analysis (which you will learn in your small business management course) you can adjust the prices as needed.

If you price this way be sure you're evaluating prices of your direct competitors. You're not up against high-volume department-store garden centers, you're competing with other local entrepreneurs who sell from the same type of location you sell from and at the same approximate volume levels.

When will I cash my first check?

Choose fast-growing annual flowers or vegetables and just weeks after the first seed is planted you should have a check in your hand. Perennials and shrubs can take from 2-5 years to grow to sellable size for retail. In extreme cases, certain trees may take ten years more. And you thought it was bad when your last employer said he had to hold back your first check for a week.

How much can I make?

There's no real limit of course; a nursery or greenhouse operation can be expanded into a large, multi-million-dollar-gross, operation. As a one man show, you can still expect to make a decent living. $25,000 to $45,000 annually is a reasonable net to shoot for. Profitable large operations provide their owners with profits measured in hundreds of thousands of dollars per year.

How difficult is this row to hoe?

The ideal situation is to find a steady sales outlet for your plants before you even begin operations. If you simply grow what you're good at growing, figuring you'll find a market later, you may have your work cut out for you.

If you grow what people want to buy, this is not a difficult business to get started in. On a scale of one to ten with one being the easiest- growing and selling plants would be a four.

* * *

The more you can learn about marketing, the better. For example, though artificial Christmas Trees have diminished the market for selling them, real, live trees are still a huge business. The sellers who do the best are the ones with a flair for marketing. They offer free sleigh rides, give away free hot chocolate and coffee, pay for an appearance from Santa Claus (and they don't skimp either, they get the *real* Santa, not those impostors you see in department stores) and in general create a fun atmosphere that brings back the same tree buyers year after year.

It's not that you must have a party every time you wish to sell a plant but good marketing techniques will attract buyers to your location. Maybe a special sale on poinsettias is more your speed or perhaps a series of soft-sell newsletters to all former clientele. Find something extra (or blitz customers with several different extras) to attract customers.

* * *

Advantages and Disadvantages

This is definitely not a mobile business. It is not portable. In fact if you have to move suddenly while you have crop growing, you may be forced to sell your stock for far less than its real value.

If you enjoy long vacations this may not be the business for you unless you take them while stock is dormant or between seasons. Plants require attention daily or almost daily in their active growing seasons.

Other disadvantages: you'll be out in the sun a great deal. Skin cancer might be a threat. Of course thousands of people work outdoors constantly without suffering anything more than an occasional sunburn. Also there is a great deal of bending and lifting required. And some larger plants require physical strength to maneuver them.

Now the good stuff: If you enjoy working with your hands in an outdoor environment, this is an occupation you might seriously consider. Most of the time growing plants is a low pressure job. It can get busy in peak season but the rest of the year you can work at whatever pace suits you.

There is a great deal of variation in the tasks you'll perform and a great deal of decision making while moving from place to place within your work area. Not only will you get exercise but the work will rarely be repetitive.

* * *

The author's landscape nursery

I entered the nursery-stock-growing business with built-in sales because I already had an established landscape operation. I had become tired of completing landscape jobs then handing over one third or so of the job's gross to the nursery. I decided to learn to grow some shrubs and trees myself. That way, I reasoned, I would either make more profit per job booked, or work less jobs and make just as much money.

The first couple years were difficult- the time taken away from other tasks to tend plants that returned zero in cash flow cut into income. But the third year started a trend of increasingly lucrative plant sales years.

I find growing plants tremendously rewarding work and love the many colors and textures the shrubs come in. The plants require a lot of care but my business is big enough now that my presence isn't really necessary most of the time anyway.

To start a landscape nursery (a nursery that sells shrubs and trees exclusively to its landscape installation customers), you must establish a landscaping business along with your plant growing enterprise. Although it seems like you're starting two separate businesses, they dovetail so perfectly, that they can be treated as one. At first there is no need to try to grow every plant you'll ever need. Just start with the shrubs you sell in quantity in your landscapes. When your plants mature, use them in the job instead of purchasing them wholesale at the local nursery.

For example, from my yellow page ad for my landscape installation business, I recently received a call from a customer needing a hill covered with plants. In this area, plants on a hillside means blue rug junipers 99% of the time.

I sold the customer on 100 blue rugs in the 2 gallon size. The wholesale price on a 2 gallon blue rug is $12, so I would have spent $1,200 on them at a nursery; however, I purchased all the rugs that I planted in that job for under $150 as seedlings and grew them to the two-gallon size. Ignoring the labor I put into growing them, my gross profit on just the blue rugs was over $1,000. I also profited from what I charged the homeowner for installation of those plants, a markup on the wholesale price to near retail, plus my 20% profit on the job. In short: I made a killing.

Starting a landscape installation business solves two major dilemmas for a home-based nursery man- 1. Who will I sell all these plants to? and...2. Will I appreciate people coming on my property to buy plants? Since your sales calls will be at other people's houses, they'll never come to yours. If they request to see plants in person, then send them to a local nursery to inspect the varieties you intend to plant, but they won't often ask to.

A landscape nursery solves most of the potential problems of growing and selling plants from home.

* * *

For Further Study:

Your local library should have a wealth of information on growing specific plants. Be careful of books that are more than a few years old. New growing techniques and new varieties of plants are constantly being developed. Not knowing about the latest disease-resistant varieties or varieties that are now grown more efficiently in soilless mixes or even hydroponically could put you at a serious competitive disadvantage right out of the starting gate.

Many of the resources in the landscaping chapter apply to this business as well but none more than the Reader's Digest Illustrated Guide to Gardening. Yes, it's that good.

The Mail Order Association of Nurseries P.O. Box 2129 Columbia, MD 21045. Members are (mostly larger) nurseries that sell plants by mail order.

Your state Dept. of Agriculture can provide you with any licensing information regarding the growing and transporting of plants.

Brighton By-Products P.O. Box 23, New Brighton, PA 15066 has a 150 page catalog of horticultural supplies for professional growers. Here you'll find pro growing mixes, fertilizers, pots, flats, greenhouses, soil sterilizers, and more. You name it, they probably have it.

Harris Seeds P. O. Box 22960 Rochester, NY 14692-2960 carries a wide variety of perennial and annual seeds.

Musser Forests, INC P.O. Box 340 Indiana, PA 15701-0340 carries many varieties of seedling shrubs and trees with volume discount pricing.

Creekside Gardens 155 Nix Rd. Chehalis, WA 98532 is a wholesale supplier of perennial flowers, woody ornamentals, and herbs.

Chapter Nine

Magazine Article and Book Writing

You open up the latest issue of Handyman Magazine. "Could this be the one?" you wonder. You flip to the Table of Contents. "Oh, wow this *is* it" you realize. Your heart is in your throat as you frantically tear to page 96. There, for all the world to see (or at least 3 million subscribers) is your byline under your first article " How to Free a Frozen Pipe Using Only Cardboard, Needlenose Pliers and a Flame-thrower."

With a mixture of fear and excitement you nervously read the article faster than a male homeowner tearing through the duct tape aisle during a blue light special at K-Mart.

You walk outside. There's Mr. Jones getting his mail. And there's Mrs. Smith, sweeping her porch. They have no idea that from this day forth, nothing will be the same. You feel like you just caught the touchdown pass that won the Super Bowl. You're now a published writer.

* * *

There are hundreds and hundreds of magazines that will review ideas from new writers. And they buy a lot of them. Millions of dollars are paid out every year by publications purchasing the right to print freelance work. The only real qualifications needed to succeed as a freelance writer are: 1. An ability to write clearly and 2. The ability to submit ideas that suit the publication.

Book publishers also abound. There are small, independent presses that publish for reasons other than purely monetary ones; huge publishing companies that only consider famous authors whose name value alone will sell thousands of copies; and all sizes in between.

If you think you know how to turn a pretty good phrase, or tell a good story, this field may be just what you're looking for.

What Is the Difference Between Magazine and Book Writing?

Writing is a form of communication and for writing to have a purpose, it must have a reader. Because the reader reads for several different reasons- to be entertained, or to learn, or to laugh, etc.- there are different types of writing.

Magazine writing is almost always tightly focused. In other words a camping magazine probably wouldn't want a general story about camping, they want in-depth articles on lesser-known aspects of camping. They'd likely pass (reject your idea) if you submit a piece titled "How to Go Camping" but might accept "25 Nighttime Camping Tips to Help You Sleep Better." The difference is: the general article is like shooting a blunderbuss full of camping tips at readers who are experienced campers and already know camping basics, whereas with the "Nighttime Tips" article you've focused that blunderbuss approach down to a 20 gauge shotgun pattern by limiting your tips to nighttime. Then you focused the idea even further by limiting the nighttime tips to ones that help you sleep better.

The Structure Is Different Too

Magazine readers often browse through an issue until an article grabs them. The first paragraph has to be interesting enough to pull in a wide variety of readers. The second or third paragraph functions as a funnel- letting the reader know what the real focus of the article is on. This "nut graph" is an important component of magazine writing, although not every article has one.

Another difference: magazine pieces contain an obvious ending unlike newspaper stories which can be clipped off anywhere to fit a certain space.

There are other factors common only to magazine articles as well but detailing them is best left to another book. Suffice it to say that writing for magazines requires a different approach than writing a book does, or even other types of articles.

Writing Books

Book writing differs from magazine writing in that it allows for writing about broader subjects than articles allow. But if you do choose a tightly-focused subject you can cover it more in-depth than you could in a magazine piece.

A book reader will usually give a book more of a chance to develop than they'll give an article. They are already interested in the subject or they'd not have selected the book. You want to hold their attention, but don't need to resort to the theatrics that magazine articles require, to focus the reader on your subject.

Why does a market exist for freelance writing?

Communication is a basic human need. Since most people are taught how to read in grade school they are quite comfortable receiving much of the information they want from a printed page.

One reason people like that information delivered in book and magazine formats is because both are convenient and inexpensive yet can convey a vast amount of information quickly. Plus, they can be easily stored and accessed again as-needed. They are also easy on the eye.

While the masses increasingly get information from computers, and computer files have many storage and editing advantages over print, computer screens fatigue most people much quicker than printed pages do. And using a computer to access information requires not just reading skills, but typing and computer skills as well. The number of computer users is increasing, but not all people have a computer or even a desire to use one.

As more people learn to use computers, it could actually produce more readers, making print books and magazines even more popular- a trend that seems to be in evidence already.

Many people read purely for entertainment. TV and home video movies have been on the scene for many years now and still for many people, curling up with a good book of fiction is the more satisfying activity.

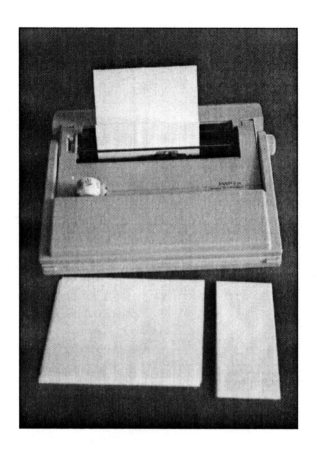

The basic tools for writing are not expensive. Stamps, an electric typewriter, paper and envelopes are all you need to get started.

The market for freelance writing exists because editors have learned that it's not only less expensive to hire freelancers than to keep huge staffs, but it also gives their publications more diversity in terms of ideas and styles which helps keep reader's interest level high, and results in more subscriptions and book sales.

Will you have to move?

Unless you wish to write for *Eastern Tennessee Auto Lover* magazine and you live in Massachusetts or want to write the book *How I Bicycled Up Mt. Everest 3,429 Times* then, no. You won't need to relocate to write.

Editors don't usually care where you live, provided you deliver a good article. Your mundane location may even be a plus. To you it may seem like a boring area but to someone who lives or edits far away, it may seem exotic. If you take the time to dig out the story ideas that exist in your area, you'll be the only logical choice to write the story if it's assigned.

* * *

My first assignment:

I'm living proof that you don't need to be a "name" writer or live in some exclusive area or "have connections" to get an assignment. You don't even need any formal training in writing- I completed several national magazine assignments before I had any training whatsoever.

When I received my first official assignment I lived in a small town in Pennsylvania, had no track record to speak of, and the only connection I had was the one that connected my boat trailer to the hitch of my truck when I went fishing. Still, there I was, just six days after I sent my very first query, listening to the editor from a big glossy outdoor sport magazine telling me that I was being assigned a 200 word article and I'd be paid 125 dollars if I could submit it by the following Monday. I was thrilled to say the least.

* * *

How much money is needed to get started?

At minimum you'll need a good electric typewriter, a good supply of stamps and envelopes, and a few reams of white paper. Buying a couple of good books on the writing craft is necessary. You'll also save yourself a lot of time and money if you buy a Writer's Market so you'll have a list of places to submit your work along with all pertinent contact information.

Using *Writer's Market* to order sample issues at $2 to $5 each, you can quickly determine if a magazine is one you even wish to write for. Once you find a mag you like, subscribe. It's cheaper than buying several samples and most editors expect you to read several issues before querying with an idea anyway. Figure $100 just for purchasing enough publications to get started. If you write books you won't need subscriptions or samples but you'll use this money to send out your book for review, purchase suitable shipping boxes and to locate and contact suitable publishers.

You'll need a lot of stamps- figure at least fifty dollars worth to start. They'll be used to order samples, send out your queries, stamp your self-addressed stamped envelopes (a must if you want a reply) and return acceptance letters to editors.

Altogether, $400 is the least investment you could make to get a serious start in this business unless you already own some items.

While it's quite possible to start a writing career or any career covered in this book without a computer, writing is a process of word manipulation. And nothing can manipulate words like a word processing program. Copy, paste, delete, reformat, and change typestyles at will; with a word processor all of that and more is simply a matter of a mouse click or two. If you can afford it, a computer with a good word processing program installed will maximize your efficiency.

March 11, 1999

Sarah Jones
Make Money Magazine
10000 Broadway, 15th Floor
New York, NY 10679

Dear Sarah,

When a potential customer calls Kris Hines or Lisa Smith asking if they are able to handle a job, they don't have many options. "We Can," they promptly reply. After all, "We Can" is the name of their 4-year-old home canning business.

The two friends started out by giving free samples to co-workers. As news of their business spread, orders began to come in. A trickle at first, word-of-mouth soon helped build a steady customer base. And their enterprise kept right on growing. Now, "No matter how much product we make," says Lisa, "We can't keep up with the demand."

Starting part-time with an investment in equipment and supplies of under $100, and with no real competition or advertising costs; Kris, 28, and Lisa, 27, were soon making a gross profit of $70 per production hour. Focusing on producing high quality product efficiently, they can and sell things like salsa, fruits, vegetables, pie fillings, and more.

In a 900 to 1,500 word article, tentatively titled **"They Can!"** I'd like to clue in my fellow readers of <u>Make Money</u> to the details regarding this profitable niche business. Where to buy supplies; that selling by the case is more profitable than by the jar; what times of year are busiest; and what types of people make the best customers are just a few of the topics that will be covered.

A good quality 35mm full-color photo or slide of Lisa and Kris in action can be supplied. A computer disk will accompany the manuscript. First rights are available and I can complete the piece within three weeks from the date of assignment.

Clips are available; however, I'm not enclosing any because you are already familiar with my work, having recently assigned me a 900 word article.

Sincerely

Mr. Hopeful

A sample query letter

Normally no more than one page, a query must present the idea for the article while showcasing your writing skill. The names have been changed but the text is exactly the same as the original query that landed the author a $275 assignment from a national magazine. The font size has been reduced from 12 to 8 so it would fit on this page.

There are also some stand-alone word processors on the market that are much cheaper than a full-blown computer. Either a computer or dedicated word processor is a huge step up from an electric typewriter.

A stand alone word processor instead of a typewriter would raise your total investment to around $600 to $800, whereas the investment in a decent home computer might require an investment of $1,500.

How much money can I make?

Everyone writes at different speeds and efficiencies. Another big consideration is how good you are at originating ideas that are right on target. If you have a 50-50 acceptance to query ratio and a writer-friend of yours is only getting 1 in 10, you'll make far more money per hour since queries pay nothing.

The best way to figure potential income is on a per word or per project basis. Most book advances to unknown writers are in the $1,500 to $5,000 range. After-publication royalties are normally 6-10%. Some are higher, but they're almost never over 20%. Often the advance is the only money a writer will see as about 80% of books published lose money. If your book is one of the 20% that "hits" then royalties can range from very little to quite substantial amounts.

Magazine articles pay anywhere from just a few cents per word at small publications (under 10,000 subscribers) on up to $1.25 or so per word. Most new writers break into a magazine with short pieces that may only pay $25 or $50 for 100 words (a paragraph or two). Also common is the 900 word article (about 1 magazine size page) at $100 for first rights (you then can re-sell the article after it's published) or about $300 for all rights (they can re-print it as often as they wish at no additional pay though you can never sell that article again).

From those humble beginnings you can work your way up the ladder to larger, longer features that pay thousands of dollars.

To accumulate a decent annual income you need to keep busy, and the work is certainly out there. One writer reports juggling up to 29 assignments at once. Another reports making a living just on book advances alone. Your ability to get your share of the work available rests almost entirely on your ability to generate effective queries and proposals.

How long will it take to get established?

Don't quit your day job to be a writer. Eventually perhaps you can, but too many novices don't take into account how long it takes to establish relationships with editors. It takes months for some magazine query-screeners just to respond to a query. How can you support yourself in the first three months of your writing career when many editors won't even respond to your queries within three months?

Realize too that after a query is accepted and you take the time to write, polish and submit the article, it takes even more time to get paid. You have to be realistic. At the same time know that: while it may take over a year to start seeing regular cash flow, a good writer often becomes well-established within two years.

There is a substantial difference between being a "good writer" and being a good magazine or book writer so there will be a learning curve as you begin marketing your work. Translation: even if you are a good writer, when you first start writing for publication you're going to get a lot of rejections before you start getting acceptances. To give yourself a fair shot, plan in advance to submit book proposals to at least 50 publishers or write at least 100 queries to magazines before you stop to evaluate your progress, regardless of what happens. It may take that long for you to figure the whole process out. And if you write 100 queries to magazines with no acceptances, you are definitely doing something wrong.

* * *

The author continues his story

When I hung up the phone after getting an assignment from my very first query I was quite astounded. "If it's this easy," I thought, "This business will be a cakewalk to master."

Well, it wasn't that easy. Fifteen more queries went out. Every few days I'd polish up another, package it carefully, and mail it out. Every time the phone rang I thought it was an editor was calling.

It wasn't.

In fact, the queries started coming back. The editors were rejecting them! How dare they! Couldn't they see how well-crafted the queries were? My feelings were really hurt. I started thinking that perhaps I was just a one-shot wonder who got lucky on the first try.

I was learning the hard way that you must follow the rules. Many of my queries had been sent to magazines that I'd never seen, let alone studied. Later when I did see them I knew immediately they weren't for me, even though the listing in Writer's Market had sounded like they were perfect.

In spite of myself I struck pay dirt again on query #16, but by then four months had elapsed since I had first started my part-time writing business. I settled in for the long haul...

My first 30 queries garnered only 4 assignments. On further analysis I realized that since those 4 assignments were from a total of two magazines, I was lucky to have 4. Had I not submitted to those two places, I'd have likely had zero acceptances in my first 30 queries; empirical evidence suggesting that you should submit 100 queries before evaluating the results.

What sells?

Non-fiction sells. So does how-to, where-to and personal experience. Diet and exercise, self-help, sports and hobbies all sell. "The Great American Novel" is difficult to make money on unless you are a well-known author. There are exceptions to that statement but in general, it's true. Some new writers do carve a niche in the fiction or poetry fields and if that's where your interest lies, don't force yourself to write something you don't enjoy. What would be the point? Just be aware it may take much longer to break into fiction markets.

Before contacting publishers, determine exactly what type of work they publish. Refer to this information as you formulate ideas and write queries.

Start small and work your way up

When you approach a new magazine, it might be wise to try to sell them a short piece, especially if it's a national magazine with a large subscriber base. They may not trust a new (to them) writer with a feature until the writer proves they understand the magazine with a short piece first. After that perhaps a "25 Tips" type article would work. How-to pieces are also a good approach for a new market.

If you're trying to get a book contract, you need to contact the publishers and get as much information as possible about the types of books they publish. Some information can be gleaned from *Writer's Market*. Many publishers also have manuscript guidelines which should be ordered if they're available. Also ask for a catalog of all the titles they currently have in print.

Compare your book idea with the types of books they publish. If yours differs substantially in terms of the intended market or subject matter, you might not want to tie up time submitting your book idea to a publisher who will probably pass. Your electronics book "How to Fix Your VCR" intended for the consumer market, probably won't be accepted by a university press that publishes electronics books intended for the classroom, for example.

If my idea is accepted, how long before I have that first check in hand?

There are four basic types of agreements you can write under which cover the time frame it takes to get paid. You could work under an advance payment agreement. Book publishers often give advances against future royalties to writers to cover living expenses during the period they are actually writing the book. If the editor is slow in reviewing your idea (and they usually are) and making a decision, it could take months to a get your first check.

A second method of payment is called "on acceptance." This means that the payment process is set in motion the day the publication accepts your work and is normally used by well-established magazines. In reality, some publications mail checks promptly (you'll have it within a week); others say they pay on acceptance but the actual process will put a check in your hand one to two months after the date of acceptance.

A third method is "on publication," which means you'll get paid sometime after the piece is printed. Short pieces and filler material often are paid this way even by name magazines. New magazines almost always pay this way for all articles. Allow up to two months beyond the publication date to actually receive your check.

A fourth method, used only by book publishers is to pay royalties on either the retail or wholesale price. This is the slowest method because payment occurs after publication (and books can take a long time to be edited and actually printed), then the books must be distributed, sold, and accounting practices must determine how much royalties are due. Finally a check is issued. If sales are expected to be minimal, publishers may only want the hassle of cutting a check once a year so your first check might take up to a year after publication to get into your hands. In rare cases even longer. Even in a best case scenario you won't see a royalty check for at least two months after publication.

How do I price my writing?

This is one creative business where pricing is easy because normally you don't set prices. If your work is accepted, the editor will offer you their standard fee based on your article's length and complexity. They will usually offer it in a "take it or leave it" fashion but you can sometimes successfully negotiate the fee upward with open-ended statements such as "I usually get more than that for an article of that length" or "I'm going to have to do a lot of research on this one, can you go a bit higher?"

If you are going to incur substantial expenses while performing the assignment, such as travel or long distance phone calls, be sure to ask in advance that they be reimbursed.

How can I have my work evaluated?

If you're just starting out, there are a number of good books on writing magazine articles and books. Buy a few and set aside a portion of each writing day to read them thoroughly. Your best means of evaluation is simply to get a good book on how to write queries, start submitting some, and let editors do the evaluating for you for free.

Editors are good judges of writing skill. If you have three or more independent sources of confirmation from editors of your talent- any mixture of three books or articles accepted for publication- you are a good writer. If you get nothing but a steady string of rejections for your efforts, you might consider taking a writing course at a local college or a correspondence course from NRI or Writer's Digest.

Good writers aren't necessarily writers who are schooled writers, however. Good writers are writers who have the intelligence to originate useable ideas and can communicate those ideas clearly.

Manuscript and Query Tips

- Keep queries to one single-spaced page (see pg. 120). Address the editor using their last name, unless it's stated in the writer's guidelines that the first name is acceptable.

- Both queries and manuscripts should have a one-inch margin at the sides, bottom and top.

- Manuscript text should be double spaced except for the heading information.

- The heading at the top of your manuscript should include your name, address, phone number, social security number, word count, rights being sold, and any other relevant technical details you wish to provide.

- Put half of the heading items in a column at the top of the left side of first page, the other half in a column at the top of the right side.

- Proof completed documents slowly, correcting misspellings.

Submit queries and manuscripts on 8 1/2" x 11" white paper. The copy must be neatly typed using an electric typewriter or a word processor. Don't submit a query to more than one editor at a time unless all parties are informed that it's a simultaneous submission. The writer's guides mentioned above are available at no charge from most magazines that accept freelance work.

It takes patience because the wheels turn slowly but if you consistently write quality proposals or queries, you will very likely break in within your first 50 submissions. As noted previously, some writers have had work accepted with their first book proposal or first magazine query.

Disadvantages

Consistency of pay can be a problem. Even if you're steadily creating work, you may go some time between pays.

Another thing to consider: most book publishers prefer authors who attend autograph parties, give interviews, and lecture. If you don't wish to participate in those types of things it could harm your chances of getting a book deal.

Most writers wish all queries were answered more expediently and paychecks were received faster. If you really lack patience this may not be the right occupation for you.

Advantages

Writing is very portable (you can write almost anywhere) and the hours are as flexible as you want them to be. The pay can be very low at first for the hours you put into your writing but it will improve and could eventually make you independently wealthy should you write a best selling book, land a syndicated magazine column or build a catalog of steady-selling work.

If you don't like working with others, this can be a solitary occupation. Then again if you do like working with people, through interviewing, selling books, and co-authoring, it can be as people-oriented as you wish to make it.

Writing can provide a bit of celebrity to the successful writer and the chance for your work to last for centuries into the future.

For Further Study

The following titles are available from Creative Books. All prices include shipping:

Writer's Market- This is an indispensable book. It has detailed listings of magazine publishers, book publishers, and other markets for writers. Contact names, pay rates, addresses, tips- it's all here. (Updated annually. The most current edition will be shipped.) $29.50

Handbook of Magazine Article Writing- A complete guide to every type of magazine article writing. Highly recommended. $17.50

How to Write Attention-Grabbing Query Letters by John Wood. The title is self-explanatory. $19.50

How to Write a Book Proposal. A step-by-step guide to the process of submitting your manuscript for publication by a book publisher. $17.50

Writing Articles About the World Around You by Marcia Yudkin. Yudkin shares her own (and other successful writer's) freelance experiences and helps you recognize article ideas in your everyday life. $19.50

Grammatically Correct by Anne Stilman. Easy, quick, and comprehensive text shows how to write concisely and clearly. $21.50

Orders for the above 6 titles should be sent to:

Creative Books
P. O. Box 463
Beaver, PA 15009-0463

Check or money order only. Money orders are faster. PA residents must add 6% sales tax. Prices include shipping and handling and the most recent edition in print will be shipped. Should a price increase occur, you will be notified (or send extra and the overpayment will be refunded). Add $10 for Canadian orders.

The Complete Guide To Magazine Article Writing by John M. Wilson. This is a book that is highly informative yet very readable. When you finish it you'll be ready to write queries or articles. Writer's Digest Books. It may be out of print but worth searching for.

The Magazine Article by Peter Jacobi. Indiana University Press. This book deals strictly with the actual writing of an article. If you can't find the publisher, the ISBN # will help you locate it: 0-253-21111-5.

Two books you absolutely can't do without: a good dictionary and thesaurus. Even if you write with a spell-checking computer you will still need to look up meanings of words. If your word processing program also has a thesaurus, there will be times when you'll still prefer a printed one as they are usually far more comprehensive. Clear writing demands simple words but you'll often use the same noun twice in a sentence, which is poor form, so you'll need a thesaurus to bail you out. You will definitely use it.

The NRI School of Writing 4401 Connecticut Ave., NW Washington, DC 20008 offers a how-to-write type course.

Chapter 10

Performing Live Music

Your fantasy is a recurring one. You're at your high school class reunion. Your classmates are boogyin' up a storm and the band hired for the occasion is jammin' like there's not gonna be a tomorrow. The weird thing is- you're not dancing, you're *in* the band. For goddsakes you can see yourself up onstage showing everyone how much you've changed since the days when you were the biggest wallflower in school. Then you catch yourself- this ain't no fantasy man, you're doin' it! You really are up onstage playing and singing and best of all... people are *diggin'* it.

Most everyone has dreams about being a famous musician or singer at some point in their life but playing music either alone or in a group can be much more than just the realization of adolescent fantasies. It's a great way to meet and interact with people- both other musicians and fans. It can become a means to make a living either part-time or full-time for the rest of your life. Many musicians are retirees who supplement social security and retirement checks with gig money. And more than anything else- music is fun.

What is Playing Live Music?

For our purposes we'll define "playing live music" as getting paid on a regular basis to play an instrument or sing in front of an audience. The definition is restricted to "playing for money" because this is a book about starting a business, not working for free.

Why does a market exist for live music?

People hire musicians for a lot of reasons. Music can put people at ease, especially if the band has a front person who is good at handling crowds. Announcements from the bandstand help an event flow more smoothly. And music is entertaining. Some people will hire a band for almost any event just because they like bands. In many of those situations, the band isn't expected to draw a crowd or make money for the person who hired them.

While there are alternatives to live music- DJ's or a jukebox to name two- live bands are considered by most people to be more interesting than "canned" music.

Where drinks are sold or admission fees are charged the hirer knows a band can put dollars in their pocket. On a good night even a smaller bar can profit by several thousand dollars after paying a band if the place stays packed all night, the band is reasonably priced and drinks are hustled properly.

Dancing to music gives singles an excuse to meet and couples a place to enjoy themselves in public. And music concerts give young adults a controlled atmosphere to get a little rowdy in.

What Opportunities are available on a local or national basis?

Every weekend there are local bands, single acts, duos and trios, playing in almost every town of any respectable size. Some bands are working weddings, some are doing parties, some are playing small bars and some are playing clubs. In nice weather there are all types of events that hire bands, from store openings to local carnivals.

On a regional level there are bands who principally play concerts- they may work a state fair one night, open for a major label act the next, and headline a regatta another night. These bands usually are paid on a higher scale than wedding or bar bands.

Of course the top-paid musicians play for major label acts. Some major-label-signed bands record and then do their own playing on the road; however, many single acts hire musicians to form a road band, leaving the players who did the studio work behind.

Studio players usually prefer recording and would be expensive to take on the road anyway. Usually these high-profile road gigs are available only if you are based in Nashville, New York, or L.A. and either respond to an audition call or more likely, are recommended by someone.

You should be aware that if you're trying to join a working band on a local level, many instruments are not in demand at all. For example, a tuba player is not likely to find a job with a local band. The only place he's likely to get paid regularly is if he's good enough and lucky enough to get a gig with a major city orchestra. Now if he swallows his pride and invests some time

in learning the electric bass- even just enough to be mediocre-
chances are he'll be working in no time as bass players are in
short supply.

* * *

A Laurie Story

What do you call someone who plays bass guitar, fiddle, acoustic guitar,
and sings? Well, "Laurie Lewis" is what her mother called her and that
worked out amazingly well considering she grew up to front a band named
"Laurie Lewis and her Bluegrass Pals." Boy, Mom either had psychic
abilities or there's some other woman with exactly the same name who's
pretty upset about the way things turned out. If that's what happened it's
understandable because Laurie not only plays multiple instruments, she also
writes songs and plays several kinds of music including jazz, old-time
country and of course, bluegrass. And let's not forget her *other* band- named
simply Laurie Lewis, with Tom Rozum and Todd Phillips.

If you think playing live music is a business only teenagers and
twenty-somethings can pull off, Laurie, a late bloomer, will change your
mind. Although she started playing classical violin at age twelve, she didn't
attempt a full-time career in live music until she was thirty-five, when she
sold the violin shop she owned at the time and took a chance on a performing
career. The move paid off- she's been voted the female vocalist of the year
by the International Bluegrass Association twice, recorded with the legendary
Ralph Stanley, and has worked on the Grand Ole Opry stage.

Her act is a good example of a concert-level group. Visit her web site at
laurielewis.com and you'll see just how much travel can be involved in this
type of band. At this writing she was following up the Snowfest in Idaho with
a concert at The Fallon Theatre in California. Then it was off to the
Anchorage Folk Festival (yes, Anchorage, Alaska), then a gig in Charlotte,
NC and on and on it goes. Many bands that work concerts travel by bus but
with jobs this far apart, Laurie and her bandmates generally fly then use a
rental van to get around.

"Only pursue music if you love it and don't mind not making it big,"
advises Laurie. She also wanted readers of this book to know how important
practice was. "There's a lot of competition out there," she says, "Find your
own voice and learn how to use it."

If you have your sights set on travelling around the country playing concerts the first step is to find a good agent (*Songwriter's Market* is a good place to start looking). Although she's based in Berkley, California, Laurie is booked by Under the Hat Productions out of Austin, Texas.

Do you have enough talent?

As long as you're not tone deaf and have a fairly good sense of rhythm there is almost surely an instrument you can learn to play well enough to join or form a group. To be a solo performer requires a slightly higher level of talent, even if part of that talent is mostly an exceptionally well-developed gift of gab. In a solo act there's no one to cover up for your inadequacies. You've got to be at least decent enough at what you do to fool most people into thinking you're good, plus handle the emcee duties.

Here are a few of the most common instruments that musicians play in paid, local, live music performances, followed by a brief discussion of what you should be able to do before you start looking for a paying position:

Rhythm Guitar: Not many bands hire strictly rhythm guitarists these days. Unless you play rhythm and sing too, you better continue your studies and learn some lead guitar also. If you do sing, then bands will hire you principally for your singing but sloppy rhythm playing could swiftly get you a pink slip.

How good you have to be depends on what you're playing. For most folk or country you should know all your open major, minor, and 7th chords and be capable of playing those as barre chords if necessary. You must be able to switch between chords quickly and smoothly. For top 40 or rock and certain types of country, you should be able to do all those things plus play fancier note and chord riffs. You also need all major 7th, minor 7th, and 9th chords. Don't get the impression from this paragraph that one type of music is necessarily less demanding than other types of music. Some genres or instruments are easier to learn than others if your goal is simply to advance to the stage where you can play a gig, but to master any type of music, or to truly master a particular instrument, is difficult. Period. Playing the right notes and making them sound authentic in a particular style of music are two completely different levels of execution.

Lead Guitar: You should know the same chords as the rhythm guitarist (you may be the *only* guitarist). You also need to know a few major and blues-based scales. Most importantly, you should be able to either improvise leads fluently, transcribe lead guitar work note-for-note, or both. Reading music is not a requirement for most bands as most groups pass around cassette tapes and each player "figures out the parts" by playing along by ear with the cassette until they can play the songs verbatim.

Bass: Knowing some scales and common chord progressions helps a lot. Certainly, you must be able to figure out bass lines from a cassette or CD and play along with it fluently.

Drums: Most drummers mistakenly think that the fancier they can play, the better they are, but they are usually the worst drummers for a band. Fancy is fine but not at the expense of keeping good time and laying down a groove. Keeping good time means to be able to play along with a metronome and stay right with it. Laying a groove means to get the basic beat of a song down pat and only put in fancy fills when there is space for them (when no one else is filling the space with their fill). And then only when something tasteful can be inserted that adds to the song.

A drummer should be able to copy beats or fills exactly from the record when requested.

Keyboards: First- be sure you have a modern synthesizer. Few groups haul around B-3's or Fender Rhodes Pianos anymore. You don't necessarily have to sing, though it's a big plus if you can. Know how to figure out parts from records, know your scales, know all your major, minor, 7th, major 7th, minor 7th, diminished, and augmented chords in all keys.

Vocals: The four most common problems with singers are 1. Lack of projection. 2. Bad tone 3. Failure to stay dead on key 4. Lack of range. You must be able to sing loudly enough to cut through the music. If you're only competing with a light piano on "The Way We Were" you will need to project just enough to be heard, but if you're trying to belt out Cindi Lauper's "Money Changes Everything" over a rock band that's kickin' out the jams you better be puttin' out sound with everything you've got. Mics can only turn up so far before they begin to squeal due to too much gain (this is called "feedback").

Your range has to be wide enough so you can sing all the songs you plan to cover in a night comfortably. Of course the band can help the situation by changing the keys of the songs to suit you.

Many people don't realize it when they are going off key (singing slightly flat or sharp). Some really, really bad singers *think* they're pretty good. But unfortunately, they're quite wrong. Taping yourself, then evaluating how well you stay on key can help you improve.

Bad tone is a subjective thing. Neil Young could hardly be considered the epitome of great tone the way a Tony Bennett or Robert Plant could be in their respective fields. If the audience makes strange faces when you sing it may just mean you'll never be a great copy singer. Perhaps your uniqueness will take you right to the top of the charts.

What's the best way to evaluate musical talent?

Well, the worst way is to listen to friends or family. Unless they regularly go to hear pro bands they have nothing valid in their frame of reference to compare you to. They may think you're fabulous only because they've never heard a true pro player or singer live.

You have a few choices here. 1. Take lessons from a teacher who is actively working the local bar circuit. They'll know if you are ready to join a band or not. This advice applies to vocalists too and is the highly recommended choice. 2. Find some local players through a music store and set up a jam session- a private get-together where musicians meet each other and play some songs together informally. 3. Watch your local paper for jams at local establishments which are public versions of the same thing. Usually no pay is involved. If you're not keeping up at a jam session, you'll be the first to know. This could be an intimidating experience for someone starting out and so is *not* a recommended choice for absolute beginners. 4. Audition for a group. You can't possibly be any worse than at least half the people who audition for groups. Of course they can't hire everyone so even if you are good enough you may fail a few auditions at first, but if you don't get some sort of serious interest after 5 or 6 auditions you either aren't good enough yet, or someone spiked your cologne bottle with rotten eggs.

How much investment is involved?

Performing can require a substantial investment in terms of time and money. You're looking at anywhere from six months to two years of at least a half-hour practice, several days each week, to learn an instrument. And sometimes longer than that. Once you are ready to join a band there's practice with the band- and most new bands will practice almost nightly for two months to prepare to play their first gig. After the first gig, they practice at least a few hours one night every week to learn new material. You'll also need to put in time on your own to learn your parts. It should be noted that some working bands do not practice.

As far as money- many singers invest in nothing more than a good microphone. A suitable mic for live use such as the classic Sure SM-58 and a mic stand to go with it will run about $150. That could be it as far as money investment goes- or it could be just the beginning.

You may find a job with a working band who lets you use their PA system (the amplifier for the vocals) or you may decide to put your own band together which means buying your own PA, an expensive endeavor. You can get a decent basic system for well under $1,000 but it would be suitable only for the smaller venue. By no means would it be considered a pro system. A basic bi-amped high-quality system complete with snake and monitors would start at around $7,000 and go up substantially from there.

For players- if you sing or plan to talk to the audience you'll need a mic and stand, and of course you need a decent instrument that stays in tune. Usually $250 will purchase a good used guitar or keyboard. Drummers will usually have to invest in drum mics. 4 mics is a good start though they can be of much lower quality than the SM-58 mentioned earlier. Starter drums themselves, suitable for using on a gig, can set you back $600-$2,000 depending on how big of a set you need. Used sets are often available.

If you play bass, guitar, or keys, you'll need an amp. Be sure to buy something with enough power to do the job you need done. A basic combo amp can be had for between $400 to $800 dollars but be sure to tell the salesman exactly what type of gigs you'll be using it on and if he says you need more power, definitely spring for the extra watts. He's not upselling you. He's trying to prevent you from wasting your money and looking like a fool.

How much money can you make?

Locally- The average pay for new local bands with semi-pro gear is about $250 per gig for a 3 or 4 hour job. In an average 5 piece band that divvies up to $50 per man. By going with less pieces new bands often make out better because many places will pay the average rate regardless of the number of players. A new three piece band will make nearly $85 each for the same 3 or 4 hour job.

The key word is new. The more established an act is and the bigger crowd they can draw, the more they are worth. It's common for local 5 or 6 piece bands to work themselves into a position where they can command $800-$2,500 per job. A few bands do even better than that. Bands that draw those kinds of crowds often (but not always) have huge PA and light systems and people to run them which means there is overhead to pay off the top for both the PA and the "roadies." Many bands are able to increase their pay substantially though without adding much overhead.

How much you'll make per year depends on how many nights you play on average each week. Full time bands generally work five to seven gigs per week.

Hotel work- "Road bands" that travel various circuits, that is they travel from one hotel to another, can make very good money. Some "circuits" are put together by independent agents and consist of a series of various hotels that are as close together as possible. For example, the band will work a Holiday Inn for three weeks then travel to a Ramada for the next three. The entire band's pay is usually about $1,500-$2,000 per week after the agent's cut. Rooms are usually free. That means your only real road-related expense is food and a vehicle. Some bands travel like this for years with no permanent home.

There are also circuits put together by hotel chains. These gigs pay a musician up to $40,000 per year.

Regional- The "state fair" level bands are almost always up in the $800- $4,000 per gig range. Overhead can eat away at even the biggest numbers and each player may only see $100-$200 per job. Some groups pay out substantially better than that.

National- Working for a major label artist is not always a guarantee of high pay if the artist has just been signed and hasn't had a hit yet. Sometimes they're still losing money and won't be buying the band members Cadillacs for Christmas. On the other hand well-known artists with a track record of hits normally measure a band member's pay in thousands of dollars per week and just maybe they *will* find a gift certificate for an Eldorado stuffed in their stocking.

* * *

A Success Story

As I was writing this chapter a piece was printed in the local paper that perfectly illustrated the point that musicians who are serious about their work and willing to relocate can indeed make good. An article in the Beaver County Times by entertainment writer Scott Tady reported that drummer George Perilli, a Beaver County native, had just been hired to drum on Reba McIntyre's then upcoming European tour.

Not long before that piece came out, Garth Brooks played a concert in the area and who was his drummer (who also received a nice write-up in the same local paper)? None other than Mike Palmer, also a native of Beaver County. In fact, Mike was drumming for Garth long before Garth was a household name.

Two of the biggest names in country music are touring with drummers from an area that has no inherent connection with Nashville, TN whatsoever so the only possible conclusion one can make is: It's quite feasible to move to Nashville and get hired by a nationally known act. That's not to say it will happen just because you move. But it can and does happen.

* * *

Doing it all yourself- If you can pull off a solo act that is entertaining enough to work gigs where you're not expected to make a profit, parties for instance, or perhaps even draw a crowd that makes a profit for an establishment, you can make excellent money gigging locally. Normally $150 and up per three or four hour performance. Singers who can't find bands can often make very good money by using a karaoke machine as a backup. Of course if you go that route you'll have to share the stage with every amateur who decides they want a share of the limelight.

Cutting overhead- will increase your pay. In most cases, the less musicians there are to pay, the more money each person receives. Technology has made great advances in the last fifteen years. Midi, drum machines, synthesizers, vocal harmonizers, and other electronic marvels permit bands to sound great with fewer mouths to feed. This is a very good thing if you are making more money because of it. It's not so great if your job is the one that's eliminated. The best thing a musician can do is embrace the technology and learn to use it to their advantage.

How long before I see my first pay?

Assuming you are competent on your instrument and ready to get serious about finding a gig, you could get lucky and see your first pay within a few days of beginning your search. You might find work "filling in" for a sick or absent player or ....

So That's a Drum Machine...

Most larger bands still use live drummers but many single acts and duos now use a little box like this one. Just tap the keys and out come realistic drum sounds.

Compact, reliable, capable of delivering perfect tempos every time and with no micing needed, drum machines have also cut into the work available for drummers in recording studios. Smart drummers have adapted by purchasing a machine, learning it thoroughly, and are in demand as programmers.

perhaps even find a steady job replacing someone who quit an already working band.

If you're not so lucky and you have to join a newly-forming group or put together your own act, it will require at least a couple months of practice time before you're going to book a paying job. And that's if a job can be found immediately. Not many employers wait for the last minute to book an act so plan on the safe side; allow another month or two before you actually see any cash.

How long will it take to get established?

Whether you're a musician breaking into a new area or a new act trying to get established, allow at least two to three years before you establish a network of steady, dependable jobs. If you're exceptionally good at drawing crowds or exceptionally good at networking though, you can become "established" within six months. Beware: many acts come "out of the chute" and set the world on fire because they're new. Once the novelty wears off they may have to weather a couple of lean years before re-establishing themselves.

How do I price my services?

Generally, when a musician is hired by an established act they are informed what the job will pay. It's usually not negotiable, at least not during the hiring phase.

When you are a new act approaching an employer the act sets the asking price. The $50 per man figure discussed earlier is a good starting point. Many bands will cut that a bit just to get a foot in the door on their first few jobs. However if your group is exceptionally talented, smaller than five pieces, has a lot of "name" talent, or has a great deal of overhead, don't be afraid to raise that price. Substantially if need be.

The author's experience

I started playing in bands professionally at the age of 16 and now have over twenty years of performing experience. By the age of 19 I had developed a reputation as the guy to call when a fill-in was needed on short notice who would learn a playlist note-for-note from tapes. Often I'd work 6 nights a week playing for three different bands each week. I've worked every type of situation imaginable from opening for major label acts, to working the hotel "road" circuit, to local gigs- both high class and low. How low? Well, a supposedly indoor job I played one winter was in a bar so rickety, I was actually getting snowed on as I played and everytime my guitar touched this strange little metal pole at the side of the bandstand I got zapped with a an electric shock. I don't think I'd even enter that type of establishment these days but back then I just figured I was paying my dues and actually enjoyed it in a weird sort of way.

Never once can I recall a time where I was hired by an act and was asked how much money I'd like to make. It was always: "We pay X amount per job." or "We make between X and X amount per job, per man." Of course after about 15 years I did start asking to be paid in dollars because you can't buy much with X's.

Playing was my very first "creativity-required" business endeavor. And I was no child prodigy. My first full year in the business I made only $600. Far from being discouraged, I was astounded to be paid at all for something I considered to be fun. So I stuck with it and within a few years I was able to purchase a house and pay it off, solely with money I made gigging.

I moved up in pay because I analyzed *why* I only made $600 my first year and discovered: everyone in my first group was a novice. We played only songs *we* liked with little regard for what other working bands were playing. As I began to figure this business out I realized that if you want to make consistent money as a musician you usually have to play what people want to hear, and that's not as much fun. Sometimes it feels a whole lot like work which is why musicians get paid for playing- because they are providing a valuable service.

If you are becoming a musician in order to play what you like to play- good luck, hopefully you will still see success. But if you are attempting to make a decent full-time or even part-time income, it's probably best to consider readjusting your attitude.

How do I market myself?

If you're a musician seeking work, search your largest local newspaper's classified section under "help wanted." Running an ad seeking employment can work as well. Many music stores have free bulletin boards where musicians can find each other. And of course, jam sessions are great places to network.

If you decide to put an act together, the yellow pages and entertainment sections of local newspapers should provide phone numbers of clubs, taverns, and other places that hire entertainment. For larger venues listen to the radio for contact numbers of state fairs and other hirers of entertainment. There are also books and mailing lists available that can help you locate paying gigs.

Advantages and Disadvantages

The best thing about live music work is that it usually takes place at night and on weekends leaving your weekdays free to pursue other things- from laying on the beach to developing another source of income. The hours are short compared to a regular job plus you get three 15 minute breaks during those few hours you actually perform.

It's a great line of work for meeting people and there are few businesses that will feed your ego so effectively as one where people sometimes cheer your every move. It's ridiculous to think of people cheering a CEO's every move- he picks up his pen (cheer), he sits back to contemplate an upcoming merger (cheer), he tosses a crumpled paper into a nearby wastebasket on the first try (big cheer)- but that's just what audiences do for talented musicians as they work.

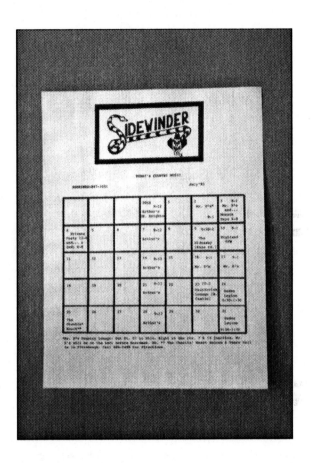

Asking fans for their address and mailing out a newsletter monthly lets fans know where you're at and will eventually build a following.

It's hard to say if the late hours musicians usually keep is a negative or a positive. It depends on whether your a night owl or an early bird. But certainly the second-hand smoke which permeates many venues is a drawback.

There is also a great deal of stress involved with being onstage. Some people handle it better than others. And if you ever make it to the "bigtime," there will almost certainly be a great deal of travel involved. Constantly moving place to place can be fun for a while but it's the rare person who doesn't eventually tire of living out of a suitcase.

How difficult is this nut to crack?

Not very. A lot of people whose talents can be described as mediocre at best break in to the local scene and at least play occasionally. By and large though, the people who work steadily on a full-time basis are talented. Many tremendously so. If you are a decent player or singer, you will eventually work your way into the live music business if you give it any type of serious effort.

For Further Study:

The following books are available from Creative Books:

Songwriter's Market- This book has one section that's indispensable to musician's trying to book a road band: detailed listings of managers and booking agents across the United States. $24.50

The Musician's Guide to Making and Selling Your Own CD's and Cassettes. A comprehensive guide to the subject. $20.50

Orders for the above 2 titles should be sent to:

Creative Books
P. O. Box 463
Beaver, PA 15009-0463

Check or money order only. Money orders are faster. PA residents must add 6% sales tax. Prices include shipping and handling and the most recent edition in print will be shipped. Should a price increase occur, you will be notified (or send extra and the overpayment will be refunded). Send $10 extra for Canadian orders.

Database America. A mailing list service principally useful to musician's because of its lists of specific types of businesses. If you're trying to market a band to associations or Fortune 500 Christmas parties, etc. these lists can make it much easier. 1-800-551-1533

Other useful books:

Making Money Making Music (No Matter Where You Live) by James Dearing. This book covers the subject in-depth. It focuses mainly on live music performing and to a lesser degree on operating a recording studio. It may be out of print but you might find it with the ISBN # which is 0-89879-101-4

Getting Noticed (A musician's guide to Publicity and self-promotion) by James Gibson. Focuses in-depth on marketing your music skills. Also possibly out of print. The ISBN # is: 0-89879-285-1

Laurie Lewis can be contacted through her web page (laurielewis.com) or through her booking agent Under The Hat Productions, 1121-B Bluebonnet Lane, Austin, TX (512) 447-0544

Chapter 11

Creative Teaching

Your student arrives at 2 o'clock sharp just like he does every Thursday. He sits down at the electronic keyboard you keep in your music room and begins to play the lesson you assigned him three weeks ago. As he plays you realize he's finally got the piece mastered. Somehow, someway the piece must have clicked for him and wow, he's really *really playing*! You think back to when he first came to you- a complete novice- and his progress is unmistakeable. He's not really a beginner any more. He's a player. And he gives you all the credit....

When student-teacher relationships have happy endings the teacher receives a tremendous degree of satisfaction out of influencing someone else's life for the better. There is also money to made in teaching someone else a creative skill they can utilize for the remainder of their life.

What is creative teaching?

The phrase "creative teaching" was coined for this chapter because no existing terminology adequately expressed what was to be discussed here. For the purpose of this book, the term will mean to teach someone a "creativity-required" skill in exchange for money. The "creativity- required" skills in this book, along with a few other realistic possibilities will be used as examples.

Why does a market exist for creative teaching?

Individuals want to learn skills for several reasons. One person may wish to pursue a career, another may simply want a hobby, some "professional students" just want to learn period, and some students may want to learn in order to gain self-esteem or for some other personal reason.

In this self-service, learn-it-all-from-a-book, paint-by-numbers society there is still a great need by many individuals for one-on-one instruction. Some students lack the discipline to study on their own. And people learn skills in different ways. Some never "get-it" unless they are able to pose questions and have them answered as they go. A one-size-fits-all program simply won't work for them.

Small children usually have difficulty utilizing self-help books as most are designed for adults. They do much better with small group or one-on-one instruction, especially if the teacher is trained to teach children. The success and proliferation of music courses designed for pre-teens such as Kindermusik (Kindermusic.com) Musicgarten (Musicgarten.org) and Schoolmusic (Schoolmusic.com) proves the market is strong.

152

Why teach?

If you're reasonably good at something, why teach? why not just do? In other words: why not play the guitar for money rather than teach?

Perhaps a drummer may indeed be good enough to perform but doesn't really enjoy it. Or maybe he can't seem to rise above the smoky-barroom scene and he's allergic to smoke. Or hates the late hours. Then again maybe he does perform and teaches nights during the week to make extra money.

Perhaps a landscaper would rather teach the craft than deal with working outdoors in a seasonal business. Or maybe he or she doesn't like doing estimates. It could be simply that the landscaper turned teacher enjoys sharing knowledge.

For most creative people, teaching is an option. It's an ace you hold in reserve should you spend the time it takes to perfect your craft only to find you don't like some aspect of the actual work. For some teachers of course, teaching itself was their target from the beginning.

What opportunities are available and where?

Teaching opportunities abound. There are writing and songwriting critiquing services. There are music teachers who specialize in one or two instruments. There are people who teach everything from horticulture to dance to art to classical guitar at community colleges. There are private lessons, small-group lessons, and full classroom situations. Most large towns and cities throughout the nation have at least some opportunities for teachers, both with and without degrees.

Relocation is usually not required although it could be if you are teaching something that is highly specialized and the students wish to learn it from a teacher or at a school located in a certain area. For example: If you wish to teach wildlife photography, your students might be better served at a school in the Rocky Mountains where grand vistas are ubiquitous and wildlife is plentiful, as opposed to a wildlife school in downtown Cincinnatti, Ohio where the scenery is less spectacular and the local wildlife consists of 18 stray dogs and 3,563 pigeons. Another example would be a recording school. Students would likely benefit the most from attending school in a major music center like Los Angeles as opposed to a facility in Kansas, although there are certainly quality recording and photography programs throughout the U.S.

Are you qualified to be a teacher?

If you are personable, have decent communication skills, have accumulated at least intermediate-level knowledge about your field, and know the basics thoroughly, you can teach beginners. It is not the teacher's job to impress students with virtuoso-level skills. The teacher's job is to impart knowledge and guide the student in the proper direction. You need to know your lesson matter in-depth enough to answer questions students may pose that are beyond the scope of that week's lesson.

The more you specialize, the less you have to know about the general field you're in. To teach horticulture requires far more knowledge than teaching someone how to grow succulents does.

To teach in public schools, colleges, universities, etc. you normally need a degree; however, in most states you can teach from your home without any special licensing.

How do I market my teaching skills?

The ideal demographic for teaching is a high-population, high-income area. Many teachers swear by Yellow Page ads. Newspaper classifieds and block ads are worth trying. Business cards left on bulletin boards and with people who might have a lot of students to refer can work as well.

If you are trying to find students to teach by mail or trying to pull students to your location from beyond your local area, try national magazines that focus on whatever subject you're teaching. Rented mailing lists (from mail list services or magazines) can work also.

Videos and books are popular methods of teaching some subjects. These are usually marketed via direct mail or through magazine ads.

Don't expect any of the above methods to work quickly or pay for themselves at first. Students will start, then some will inevitably quit. The few who stay for the long haul will be the nucleus of your business. As you accumulate more and more "stayers" you will eventually break even on your investment then finally begin to profit.

What kinds of things can be taught for money successfully?

One-on one vocal lessons are popular. Certainly music instrument lessons are mainstays of the private-lesson teaching profession. Guitar, piano, and drums are popular but to a lesser extent practically any musical instrument has some type of market. A few markets are too small to pursue but often if there's a small demand and few teachers, the price can be raised to make lessons quite profitable.

Writing and songwriting can be taught successfully, though it helps if you have some proof that you are knowledgeable in the form of clips, books, or songs you've had published. There aren't usually enough interested students locally, except in major music centers, so mail order would be the most logical method.

Photography can certainly be taught successfully as private lessons, especially popular are specialties such as underwater or wildlife photography.

Landscaping and horticulture are popular subjects but are often broken down into more specialized areas and are sold most often as books or videos on specific landscaping tasks or specific plants.

Recording Studios may find a few students locally but would be unlikely to find enough students to make teaching the main income unless additional students are found regionally or nationally through direct mail and/or magazines.

Painting and dancing are two subjects not covered in-depth in this book that can certainly be taught successfully from home. Most often, these are taught in small group lessons.

* * *

A Success Story

Frank Winter, who has taught tap, ballet, jazz, and American ballroom dancing in California for the past 43 years was kind enough to allow his story to be shared in this book. Frank had been dancing quite some time when in 1956, the opportunity to teach at a local Arthur Murray's Studio came up. He jumped at the chance to get paid for doing something he enjoyed and eventually decided to make a career of teaching dance. After a few years Frank opened his own independent dance facility, Dance America Studio, in Chico, Ca. According to Frank, "The main pitfall to avoid is to start teaching before you are fully qualified. This becomes a detriment not only to you but also to your students who might find it hard to learn and think it's their fault."

In Frank's mind he's still 21 years old and credits dance with keeping him young in mind and spirit, not to mention physically. "Many of my contemporaries," says Frank, "can barely tie their shoes while I regularly perform stretches and exercises that would permanently cripple most people my age."

Would Frank recommend teaching dance as a career choice? "Absolutely," he says "If the (teacher) is dedicated to the task of self-development and a life long learning process to stay abreast of the constantly changing world of dance."

* * *

How do I price my service?

Private lessons are not difficult to price. Group lessons generally run $10 to $20 per lesson. The more students who show per lesson, the more you make. Private lessons generally start at $10-$15 per half hour. If any ongoing expenses occur such as tapes, books, etc. they are charged to the student above and beyond the lesson fee. Some teachers carry up to 70 students per week. And certainly well-known teachers with a substantial local or national reputation can command fees as high as the market will bear.

To make money as a teacher you absolutely must set a firm pay-in-advance policy and a firm cancellation policy. Students are then charged for the time whether they use it or not. Otherwise you'll have so many cancellations you'll never make money. Don't be afraid to drop students who are slow to pay and replace them with (hopefully) better payers.

How much money will I need to invest?

If you're willing to work from a spare room or even your living room, your main expense and often the only large expense will be the promotion. The best method of advertising is to keep ads running steadily for as long as possible and as many of them as you can afford. Translation: Run the cheapest classifieds that get your message across, in as many places as possible, for as long as it takes to develop your steady clientele.

For example: if you call the two largest newspapers in your area and find classifieds are $30/ month in a weekly paper, and $30 per week in the daily, budget $1,800 for advertising start-up costs for the first year to cover both papers. Of course you can pay as you go and if the ads are even mildly successful much of the money will not come out of your pocket, especially toward the end of the first year. Often you can get steep discounts if you commit to a long-term ad upfront.

The important thing is to continue advertising for an extended period even though it may lose money in the first six or eight months. $1,800 sounds like a lot to pour into advertising but it's not a lot to risk to get a good-paying business off the ground.

Renovations to your home may be necessary. If you don't like the idea of students walking through your kitchen to get to your photography studio, you might need to put in a separate entrance. In some cases redecorating might be necessary to improve the environment so students will feel comfortable or to project a certain image.

Before undertaking expensive alterations it may be wise to bear with the current conditions until you're sure your business is going to work out. On the other hand waiting may not be possible. If conditions are so poor that the student feels very uncomfortable- there is no door on the room and your student has to practice his tuba while your daughter's Girl Scout troop makes wisecracks from the adjoining room- he won't be back and your chances of building a business are zilch.

How long before I see my first pay?

Market yourself aggressively and in most cases you'll have cash in hand within four weeks, and often the very first week.

* * *

The author's advice:

I started giving guitar lessons shortly after I started working in bands. People who knew I played often asked for lessons plus a bandmate who worked at a music store referred students to me so I really had no ad costs at first, and still was able to charge top dollar and get it. Later when I wanted more students I had to use ads.

In my early days of learning the guitar and banjo, I took lessons on each of those instruments so I had a good grasp of how a lesson was conducted and what the student wants.

One lesson I had was in a rock guitarist's home after responding to a classified running in the local paper. After we met he proceeded to give me a one hour "lesson" which was really a concert of him playing (and singing too). I left feeling like I had been ripped off and had learned absolutely nothing.

A student wants to learn, not be impressed or intimidated by the teacher's skills. I no longer teach (only because I don't have time for it) but here are some tips I accumulated while I did that will serve you well when you give lessons:

1. Be punctual. The student may be late but if you are late and the student is on time he'll feel cheated.

2. Be prepared. Whatever type of lesson you're teaching you should have an outline prepared in advance. The outline should contain each point you wish to cover. Any diagrams you'll need should be drawn in advance. Any books or supplies should be at your workstation ready to go. If you fumble around for 5 minutes hunting pens and paper, then waste another 5 minutes drawing a diagram to illustrate a point, that's one third of a half-hour lesson wasted. Plus while you're drawing diagrams, the student is bored. Hmmm...A boring rip-off....how long do you think that student will keep coming back?

3. Do not "show off." A student doesn't care how great his teacher is. At best it makes the student want to jump ahead and "learn the good stuff" at worst it makes the student feel you're wasting time or looking down on him. Your abilities will be apparent as you get deeper into the lessons when they'll be displayed as a natural course of the lesson plan.

4. Don't try to give the student too much at once. This was my main downfall. I wanted the student to feel they'd received their money's worth. They did. But they also felt overwhelmed. You can ask students if you're giving them too much, but not all students will level with you. They may not even *know* if you're giving them too much so...watch for signs: only part of the assigned work is being practiced at home, or the student seems to be getting confused a lot or there's not enough time in the lesson to both review last week's stuff plus get to this week's.

Go slow. You don't have to give a student something new each week. Give them time to master the last lesson before assigning much more.

5. Books are essential to many teachers but some, myself included, prefer to give students homemade lessons. These custom lessons can be reproduced on a copy machine and used for future students. If you have access to a computer you can make up some extremely visually-appealing lessons incorporating graphics, color, and interesting text styles.

6. End the lesson on time. Going over allotted time may seem like you're giving "extra" but to many students, especially children, a half-hour already seems like a long time. Once again, boring them will make them not want to return.

How Much Can You Make?

Theoretically you could book 80 students per week in half-hour slots. At ten bucks a lesson that's $40,000 a year and at $15/lesson that's $60,000. In reality it's usually difficult to stay fully booked and even if you have a good pay-in-advance policy it's difficult to keep it 100% enforced. How bad is it? Up to half of your available time won't be billable so your $15 per-half-hour lessons may only gross $30,000. And to keep even that many students booked, it's going to take a good amount of advertising. If you clear $25,000, you're doing well. Of course if you have a degree or are a popular performer who can get $25 or $30 per half-hour lesson, you can double that.

160

How long will it take to get established?

It takes time to build a roster of dependable students. It's unlikely to happen in less than three to six months and could take up to a year or more. Teaching is not difficult to break into though. There always seems to be at least a few people who are actively looking for a teacher at any given time. If you have the desire and the ability to stick with your plan, you're very likely to succeed, if not full time, certainly part-time.

What are the advantages and disadvantages?

It's difficult to make teaching from your home a 9-5 business. Many students will need evening or weekend hours. There's a bit of stress involved too- trying to keep your cool when a student cancels a lesson at the last minute, constantly dealing with a high turnover rate and meeting new students often. You might find you don't like a lot of strangers coming into your home. Or you might not be good at dealing with people one-on-one which is an essential skill for this business. Of course teaching by mail or through books could eliminate many of the aforementioned problems.

The advantages are as numerous as the disadvantages- many people who can't deal effectively with audiences can handle one-on-one teaching quite well. The start-up costs are low compared to many business situations and can be paid for as you go in most cases. Teaching is not as isolated as say writing or photography can often be. It's also a cash operation. You won't have to wait as long for payment as you would with plant growing or self-publishing, and you'll get paid before you do the work rather than long afterwards.

For Further Study

Your local library should have a well-stocked section on general teaching.

The following two books are available from Creative Books:

Homemade Money by Barbara Brabec. details exactly how to start, manage, market, and multiply the profits of a business at home. A good book to have, though it's not specifically about teaching. $23.50.

Making Money Teaching Music- Geared to building a successful, lucrative teaching business. While the emphasis is on music teaching, much of the information could be applied to any "creativity-required" business. $20.50 will bring a copy to your doorstep:

The above two books can be ordered from:

Creative Books
P. O. Box 463
Beaver, PA 15009-0463

Check or money order only. Money orders are faster.
Prices include shipping and handling and the most recent edition in print will be shipped. Should a price increase occur, you will be notified (or send extra and the overpayment will be refunded). PA residents must add 6% sales tax. Add $10 for Canadian orders.

If you're interested in dance lessons or learning more about teaching dance, Frank Winter (interviewed earlier in this chapter) can be contacted at: Dance America Studio, 932 W. 8th Ave., Suite R, Chico, CA 95926 or phone him at 530-342-9933.

The next two books are about teaching specific subjects:

Guitar Shop: A Beginner's Guide to Learning Lead and Rhythm Guitar by Bill Watson. Has handy checklist to track each student's progress, plus free downloadable tracks at a special website to aid student's in learning improvisation. ISBN: 0-9670751-8-1. Available at Amazon.com. Discounts for multiple copies available are from the publisher.

The Art of Teaching Writing by Lucy Calkins. ISBN: 0435088092. Details how to work students through the various stages of writing and gives hundreds of samples of student writing.

Teaching children is big business. Even if you don't focus on them, you can count on having at least a few pre-teen students:

The Magic Pencil: Teaching Children Creative Writing Peachtree Publishers. ISBN: 1561450456.

How Children Learn by John Caldwell Holt. ISBN: 0201484048.

This book is out of print but you may find it in your local library:

Freelance Teaching & Tutoring: How to Earn Good Money by Teaching Others What You Know by John T. Wilson.

Chapter 12

Songwriting

Do you dream of the day when you're listening to the radio and the DJ starts playing a special song out of the blue. It sounds professional, it's catchy, and you happen to know it's been moving steadily up the charts. But none of that is what's making your pulse quicken. None of that is what's making you feel like you're rounding the final turn at the Indy 500 with every car in the race somewhere behind you and nothing in front of you but wide open spaces and checkered flags.

What's pushing your excitement meter to nine and a half on the ten-scale is the fact that it's *your* song that's blasting from the radio. And the weird thing is- hardly anyone knows it but you....

Songwriters are a strange breed. They slave in some tiny room somewhere, often for years to perfect something that is intangible, inedible, and completely infusible. (If you don't know what infusible means, don't feel bad, the author had to look it up too. P.S.- it's a waste of time.) And what is their reward? Not money, for if that was where their satisfaction came from they'd have quit long ago. Not fame, for outside of the small songwriting community, few people will likely know their name. So what drives them? Mostly the satisfaction of knowing they've been able to achieve one of the more difficult endeavors in the creative world- they've composed a great song.

What is songwriting?

Songwriting, loosely defined, is placing a series of words on the framework of original music. For the purposes of this chapter we'll refine that definition a bit more: as either composing the lyric part or the music part of a musical work intended to be recorded by a vocalist and musicians then sold at a profit to the general public.

Writing a lyric is not difficult at all. In fact, you can write a lyric easier than the Rain Man could win a match-counting contest. But to write a professional, crafted lyric? Well now...that's a completely different story.

Professional lyric writing entails generating a lyric "concept," or idea, which is usually also the title of the song. Verses and a chorus that support the concept are then written. Sometimes a bridge part or climb (also called a pre-chorus) is needed also.

In a pro lyric clichés are deleted and fresh lines are substituted for them. Clever phrases are then worked into the body of the lyric using techniques such as metaphor, simile and alliteration to help the lyric stand out in a listener's mind. Writing a lyric is painstaking, exacting work with little or no margin for error. If you can't find a proper rhyme for a certain word in the chorus or a line just doesn't work no matter how many ways you've tried to say it, often the only alternative is to scrap the lyric and start fresh.

Writing the music isn't any easier. Any competent musician can dash off a melody. But to construct a compelling, catchy melody with proper phrasing, twists that hold a listener's interest, and most of all a hook that prospective buyers can't get out of their heads until they run to the record store and purchase the song is extremely time-consuming.

Often a songwriter (of music, lyrics, or both) will be interviewed and you'll find that they dashed off their last million-seller in fifteen minutes. Invariably they were able to do that because of the many years they spent practicing their craft in anticipation of the day when a "perfect" idea popped into their heads and they "miraculously" developed it in minutes. Yes, "15 minute hits" happen. But few writers can duplicate the feat very often, if ever again. If you're looking for an "easy, high paying," job, forget songwriting. It's best reserved for those who write songs because they love writing songs and could not imagine doing anything else with their life. Few others will have the necessary determination to stick out this difficult business.

Why is there a market for songs?

Rhythms and melodies have been a part of the human experience for as long as humankind has existed. Wind, waves, rain, a mother's heartbeat, birds singing, and whales crying are all just a small portion of the many examples of rhythms and melodies that exist in nature. They are woven into the human experience and allow music to move people on a deep emotional level.

Most people love music and listen to it constantly- in movies, as background noise, as a comfort, to liven up a party, to dance to, to listen to as they "sort out" their feelings about things. And they certainly purchase it. The selling of music is a 12-billion-dollar-a-year industry.

You'd think enough songs have been written by now that they could just be endlessly recycled... remake after remake... old songs recorded by new artists, but that's not what's going to happen.

Some songs will be re-made but not most. The public craves fresh music and teens will accept remakes of some of the music their parents grew up with but they want their own stuff too. Plus new events, inventions, fads, and people come onto the scene of contemporary culture and practically demand to be written about.

Most artists prefer breaking onto the music scene with a fresh, new song they can establish their own identity with rather than a song already associated with some other artist. There's also a lot more money to be made if an artist records a new song through their own publishing company. And some songs are recorded so perfectly by a prior artist that it's considered to be the "definitive" version- the best it can possibly be done. Few artists want to tackle a song if they are risking being compared unfavorably to an artist who recorded it previously. Another big factor is that new technology and recording techniques make songs recorded just a few years ago sound dated. If you have to record anyway to take advantage of better technology, why not record something new?

Where are the opportunities?

Few books on songwriting will tell you the plain hard truth because it could hurt their future book sales to songwriters if they level with you, so they focus on what's possible instead of what's realistic. Here's the real deal:

If you are trying to make songwriting your career and you write and perform rock or top 40 you are best off to move to a major music center, either L. A., Nashville, or New York City. Those areas are where the people you need to network with are. That's where people who have the power to sign your songs and offer you staff writer positions are. If you write country music or don't perform, Nashville may be your best choice. Nashville takes non-performing songwriters seriously.

If you can't relocate, there are other ways to succeed as a songwriter including 1) Develop a career as an independent artist. 2) Function as a songwriter/manager for a local act and guide their independent career to the top, first with regional hits, then leverage that track record to sign with a major label. 3) Submit songs to music publishers by mail. It's rare that a song submitted by mail becomes a hit but it *can* and *does* happen (and you'll soon be reading about one of those one-in-a million success stories). 4) Align yourself with a local music publisher who's getting significant chart action.

The independent career path mentioned above is a very reasonable choice. In fact, I have to look no farther than my own household for a major success story. My wife, Rhonda Watson, released her first independent CD in 1997, promoted it relentlessly (mostly on the Internet) and by 2001, had released several other CDs and obtained significant airplay in Europe.

In February of 2001, she performed on the main stage of Europe's largest country music fair in Berlin, Germany, and at the time of this writing, has a European tour scheduled for August and September of 2001 for a personal in-pocket-net of up to $1,100 DM ($550 U.S.) for a two hour show, significantly more than what she makes in the U.S. You don't necessarily have to go overseas to develop an independent career, but you must invest substantial time in your dream. Most people who succeed in any facet of the music biz first work very hard, long hours promoting, marketing, giving interviews, etc. for low or no pay. They don't passively wait to be discovered!

You may be wondering- if new songs are so "in demand" why don't publishers swoon over new talented writers wherever they find them. There can't be that many people who write songs, can there?

Think again. There are thousands and thousands of active songwriters at any given time. And they are all competing for a shot at the top 40 charts which turns over only so many times a year. So let's say you write country (since that's what the majority of writers choose to write). Well, there are probably at minimum 10,000 other country writers competing for the few hundred slots that open up on the charts every year. And the majority of those slots get filled by: 1. Self-contained singer-songwriters signed to major labels who won't do outside songs. 2. Established publishers. 3. Established writers.

Granted, most of those 10,000 writers have about as much talent as an end-table but they certainly clog things up for good, new writers (they all think they're good, new writers). And worse, publishers are so harassed by all these writers they soon adopt an attitude of "songwriters are a dime a dozen" (a belief they quickly abandon if you can put a true "hit" song on their desk. But until you prove you're more than just another unknown songwriter, don't expect the royal treatment by any means).

The Demo Is Everything

When you're ready to cut demos- spend what it takes to make a decent quality one. If the price is under $200 for a full-band demo, you are probably wasting your money. Cheap demo services are no bargain. You're almost guaranteed to receive a semi-pro job because at that price, there's no way the service could afford anything but the cheapest musicians, singers and equipment. You're doing yourself no favor if you "save" $60 but cost yourself a contract. While some article and book writers may hedge their bets by saying "a full-band demo is no guarantee of getting a cut," they say that so they don't encourage amateurs to waste money on expensive demos that will go nowhere.

* * *

The author's point of view and why.

I've heard the argument advanced by some publishers- "I'd rather see a songwriter do a good guitar/vocal demo, then if I need to order changes I don't feel guilty about 'ruining' their demo."

Now think about that... Wouldn't you be darned thrilled if a major publisher thought enough of your work to call you and request a change in order to make a song you wrote suitable for contracting, even if it meant your $300 full-band demo was wasted? Big deal! And I'm telling you based on 5 years of experience screening and signing songs at Listen Again Music-publishers are almost never going to respond to your guitar/vocal demos!!!!!

I'm not going to give advice based on *preventing* songwriters who stink from wasting money. My advice to songwriters who aren't good at writing is-get the heck out of the songwriting business! For those of you who attack this business professionally- you've read Sheila Davis' book *The Craft of Lyric Writing* and know about specific lyric techniques like alliteration, inner rhyme, and metaphor and apply them; you know it will take a serious investment of time and money in demos before you start seeing hits; and you are committed to developing a career over a period of years not months- in short you have a pro attitude. Then do pro full-band demos!

As a publisher I often wrote to or called songwriters I wanted to sign single song contracts with. Never once did I get into a bidding war over a one-instrument and vocal type demo. But top-notch sounding demos with good tight writing? That was another story. As a publisher the really good stuff just jumps out of the speakers at you. You can't ignore it. And neither can other publishers. So a bidding war starts or often never even starts because the writer has already signed the tune. Wouldn't you like to be that writer? Then do great demos!

Do You Have Songwriting Talent?

Music is such a subjective thing. What one publisher may reject, saying "I don't hear this as hit material" becomes a hit song next year for another publisher. For that reason it's difficult to see how any one person could evaluate your songwriting abilities except within their own narrow view of what "good" songwriting or "correct" songwriting is.

If you are going to try to get signed as a self-contained act (one that writes all its own material, records it, and performs it) especially in alternative, rock, rap and other markets you might get away with knowing little about the techniques of good traditional songwriting and still make gold albums.

The more you're geared to landing outside songs- songs you're trying to convince other artists to record, hoping they'll make hits out of them- the more you better know about traditional song crafting technique. Certainly it can't hurt you to "know the rules" anyway, even if you intend to break them later.

The worst people to listen to when it comes to evaluating your songwriting talent is friends, fans, family, or people in the music business who never advanced beyond the local level. Those people mean well when they compliment you but they aren't qualified to make statements like: "Someday you'll be on TV, I just know it" or "You're better than what I hear on the radio. You should have a recording contract." You may well be better than what's on the radio but those artists on radio have a career and name they've built over decades. They also have clout with radio, and fans who buy their records by the millions. They can release a song half as good as yours and still sell a million times more of their songs than you can of yours. Get this through your head: The music industry isn't a talent contest, it's a CD-selling contest! Your songs will need to be far more crafted than most of what's on the radio for you to have a chance of making it.

Submit your songs to industry professionals. They are not perfect evaluators but they are the most knowledgeable people available since they deal with original music daily. Any positive comments you glean from them are extremely valuable and contract offers should be considered a validation of your talent. Because they'll be reviewing your stuff for their own needs, they'll have a very narrow focus. Therefore, negative comments should be considered as somewhat meaningless unless you hear the same comments from two or three different industry sources. Then you can decide if the comment is valid or if you're just submitting to the wrong places.

Are You Professional Enough?

When you submit work to an industry pro, the demo has to sound almost as good as what you hear from a cassette purchased at a record store. The arrangement doesn't need to be as elaborate or the playing quite as fancy but the basic sound has to be in the same ballpark. Pro songwriters submit one to three songs on short-length bulk cassette tapes loaded with quality TDK high bias tape or the equivilant. Don't use cheap off brands or submit one song on a 60- minute Maxell.

If you are forced to submit by mail, use store-bought, padded mailing envelopes to send demos. Type everything-cassette labels, addresses, letters- with at least an electric typewriter. Manual typewriters just don't get it anymore. Hand-written labels spell one thing- amateur.

Computer-printed labels can be used to advantage but don't overdo it either. Too-fancy letterheads, the need to call yourself "freelance songwriter" if you haven't had hits yet, or super elaborate packaging can make you look amateurish. Think: totally professional yet basic.

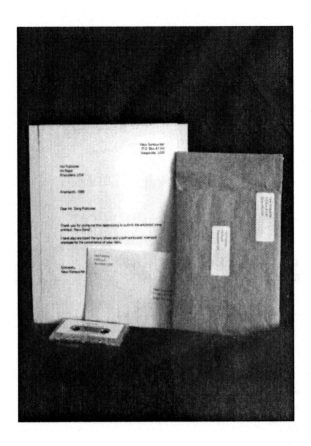

A PRO DEMO PACKAGE

Bulk cassettes loaded with high quality tapes are the way to go for submitting demos to music industry professionals. Although you may have to order 50 or 100 at a time, they can be ordered in the length you need and are less expensive than name brands; cost less to mail since they weigh less; and with the right computer software you can make typeset labels for a pro look.

A typed cover leter and lyric sheet make a better impression than handwriting. Do not hype yourself- it's the mark of an amateur...and don't forget a #10 SASE or postcard.

Always include a stamped, self-addressed envelope with every letter or package you send out. Pro songwriters don't want the actual tape back, they'd rather have it filed for future use. Publishers usually call only if they want to sign a song so a letter-size SASE provides for feedback.

* * *

A Success Story

In spite of all the previous advice about how difficult it is to get songs signed by mail, it does happen. In fact, songwriter Kristy Jackson actually experienced the very thing every songwriter who drops a song package in a mailbox dreams of: a big hit with a major artist. She not only obtained a hit through the mail, but by owning her own publishing rights, she probably doubled her income from the song.

If circumstances force you to approach publishers by mail, Kristy's experience should be inspiring. When asked to contribute to this book, she quickly responded by writing up her own story:

"I was singing and playing keyboards in a beach and Motown band in North Carolina back in '90 and I had written *Take It Back* for our band. We released it as a single in the Carolinas and it became a regional hit.

A DJ at the time had contacted me and asked if he could mail it to Starstruck (Reba McEntire's production company in Nashville, TN) because he felt it could be a hit for her. I thought to myself, "Hey, I need all the help I can get having spent years mailing tapes to numerous trash cans all over the world. What's one more!" Would you believe not only did Starstruck receive the tape but they listened to it and evidently liked it because she (Reba) recorded it and released it as the first single off her "It's Your Call" album. I had established my publishing company a few years prior to that and retained full publishing of the song. It's a one in a million story. The truth is: God smiled on me in a big way! I still live in North Carolina but now I'm able to maintain a residence in Nashville where I spend one week out of every month writing, co-writing and pitching my company's (Fever Pitch Music) catalog. Life is good."

How much investment is required to get started in songwriting?

Your first step should be to invest in a book on the overall business such as *The Craft and Business of Songwriting*, by John Braheny. Also mandatory are a copy of *Songwriter's Market* and if you write lyrics *The Craft of Lyric Writing* by Sheila Davis. A songwriter's rhyming dictionary is a good choice too.

Those books should cost under $100 if you purchase all of them and are the only required investment for the first year as you learn and practice the craft. Don't invest much in demos at this point, it's probably a waste of money. You'll write better songs later.

After you've studied the books thoroughly and have completed twenty or thirty songs *then* it's time to select the most commercial song for your first demo. If you can't produce your own full-band demo including a pro lead vocal, drums, bass, guitar and keyboards that sound professional then you'll have to hire someone to produce your demo.

At this point you need deep pockets because it's unlikely you'll get much action on your first few demos. It's time to pay your dues: Each demo will run between $150-$350 each so every set of ten demos would run between $1,500 to $3,500. Of course that cost will be paid out over a period of time.

In general, mail order demo studios are the best choice. They're almost always less expensive than local studios and producers for comparable quality because they focus only on demos. Volume allows them to price low and keep their production skills honed. A top quality $120 per hour local studio is where you want to go when you need airplay-quality master productions.

To make copies of your demos you can either purchase two good quality cassette decks (Teac makes several suitable semi-pro models) or one dubbing deck. Stay away from consumer-grade decks. The quality is just too poor and lousy copies could ruin your career. Another choice is to pay your demo service or a tape duplicating service to make your copies.

You'll also need a good electric typewriter or a computer for typing cover letters, cassette labels, etc. Figure $350 for a typewriter and a decent copy deck.

If you attempt to market your songs long distance in spite of the advice given earlier in this chapter then you have to take mailing costs into consideration. You can lessen the costs greatly by mailing three demos per package. By going with three or four songs per package you'll cut your mailing costs to 1/3 of the cost of mailing each song separately. You'll need to get each song to at least 50 industry pros to have much chance of success so you must allow $200-$300 for stamps, bulk cassettes, and packaging materials for each group of ten songs. Once again those costs will be spread out over time.

As you can see, marketing your work can be expensive- as high as $3,800 for your first ten songs and certainly no less than $1,500. The best way to make this business affordable is to spend a lot more time writing songs than doing demos or marketing. If you write 30 songs per year and attempt to demo and market all of them your bill will run into thousands of dollars each year. But if you write thirty and market only one of them your song marketing bill can be just a few hundred dollars per year which is affordable to just about anyone. For most people simply putting a stop to eating at fast-food restaurants and putting the money into demos instead would probably make them a huge success within a year or two. Uh....that's a joke, ok?

The point is: setup a writing and marketing plan you can afford to continue year after year. This is one race where the tortoise will beat the hare every time.

How much money is there in songwriting?

A monster #1 hit can set you up for life. Particularly if it becomes favored by "oldie" radio stations and/or is re-released by other artists and/or is used in commercials or movies. One song can mean lifetime riches. But many successful songwriters have a career based on a series of lesser hits.

* * *

Obtaining the right information is vital to getting anywhere in this industry. Without a mentor or books to guide you, you'll waste far too much time trying to invent wheels that other people have already ridden successfully. In fact, without solid information, you may *never* figure out this complex business.

* * *

Michael O'Connor, the publisher of several Billboard-charters, detailed his income from several songs in his 1987 self-published book *The Michael O'Connor Newsletters*. Michael reports that the Dr. Hook song "Girls Can Get It" which peaked at the Billboard Hot 100 #34 spot earned approximately $28,000 in performance income and about $45,000 in mechanical income plus another $1,500 in print and miscellaneous income.

Performance income (paid by BMI or ASCAP) is identical for the publisher and writer while mechanical and other income is split between them. If you had written "Girls Can Get It" with no co-writer your take would have been in the neighborhood of $50,000. Had you written the Michael O'Connor-published Crystal Gayle song "You Never Gave Up On Me" your share would have been over $80,000. "You Never Gave Up On Me" peaked at #5 on the Country Hot 100.

Many songs; however, that only make the lower rungs of the Billboard Top 100 ladder return a writer's share of $5,000 or less.

* * *

Forty Years of Songwriting

Lenny Green has been writing songs since 1957. His first big break came when Floyd Cramer recorded his song "Father Time" for RCA records which eventually led to him obtaining a staff-writing position with Acuff-Rose Publishing (now Opryland Music). Since then he's had songs recorded by a wide range of country artists, from the Texas Playboys to Don Gibson. His songs have been released on major labels such as CBS, Capitol, Warner Brothers, and RCA. His "Love's Got A Way" was introduced on the old Johnny Carson Show by Pat Boone while more recently his "Slow Country Dancin" was performed on the 1981 Academy of Country Music Awards show by artist Judy Bailey. Few songwriters can claim such a lengthy or more successful career.

Lenny was gracious enough to not only give an interview for this book, but he made it quite a candid one as well, as you're about to read:

Watson: Lenny, Do you think it's better if a songwriter relocates to Nashville or L.A.?

Lenny: "It most certainly increases your chances of selling your song if you can do it in person."

(Author's note: Lenny wanted to mention that there are some charting publishers outside the major music centers that may be worth pursuing if you can't get to the major music centers.)

Watson: What's your advice on demo quality?

Lenny: "Anymore you really have to produce it for them....if you don't, they can't "hear" it. This doesn't mean you have to spend $2,000 per song. Do as many do- use a songwriter demo service. For anywhere from $200.00 to $350.00 you can have a demo you'll be proud to play."

Watson: Has songwriting earned you a full-time income?

Lenny: "It did for a few years, and when it no longer did, I pursued other employment to sustain my writing habit."

Watson: What benefits or rewards have you gained through songwriting that you couldn't have gained any other way?

Lenny: "The creative process is rewarding in a very special way- you get to be in total control of the outcome of what you're creating. It teaches you discipline and that satisfaction is the benefit. It has to be ranked up there with having a son or daughter born...and they've always said that a songwriter's songs are like their children: you give birth to them, "raise" them, and you try to find a place for them in people's lives."

Watson: What advice would you give to someone who wants to pursue a songwriting career?

Lenny: "Understand from the beginning that your chances of being another Willie Nelson are slim at best. You have to beat out the best songwriters in the business to get on that CD; so you'll want to be sure and have a solid source of income while you're doing it. But the satisfaction of writing a great song, and hearing it happen in the studio can't be surpassed (unless it's when you hear it played on the radio for the first time).

When what you heard in your mind becomes real it's like a dream coming true. And worth all the effort and the hours and the days and the weeks you put into it. Last: be prepared to become addicted. It becomes who you are, not what you do!"

* * *

How long will it take to get that first check?

In a word: years. At least from the time you first start writing. It's unlikely you could get a song onto a major label album in less than one year and if you could, it may take the artist another year before they promote the song sufficiently to obtain action on the charts. Then there's the time lag of actually getting paid from your publisher or performance rights organization. Assuming a best case scenario, allow two to three years from the day you start writing songs to see your first check. In most cases it's a lot longer than that.

There are two ways around that time lag: 1. Advances received as a staff writer. If you can convince a publisher to hire you as a staff writer, you'll receive your first check within a few weeks of being hired. 2. Doing everything by yourself. Selling your own CD or cassette can put money in your pocket almost immediately after release, which brings us to our next section:

Self-releasing material

If you wish to bypass the major-labels and publishers altogether you can always release your own songs. These projects often lose money but certainly there are many examples of songwriters successfully self-releasing material, then either building a career with a number of releases or eventually getting signed based on the strength of their sales. The country group Alabama, one of the biggest names in the business, and The Kentucky Headhunters, who were popular recently, both started out with self-released albums. Your chances are best if you can expose product through a combination of live-performances, local radio, an Internet web page, and possibly even direct mail or space ads in magazines, but know that paying for advertising is very risky in this particular business. Although country groups are mentioned here, this is a viable alternative for any type of music.

Playing your songs live is the surest method of gaining sales. Performing songwriters know they can sell cassettes or CDs at gigs almost guaranteed if they have a following. If you're a non-performing songwriter who wants to self-publish you can still move product via live performance- if you can convince a working group to perform your material.

Watch your local papers for advertised gigs of local groups. Attend performances and give each bandleader a good full-band demo of at least three of your tunes. Hopefully they will be interested in developing a mutually beneficial relationship that includes performing, selling and recording your music.

Can this work? Absolutely. One non-performing songwriter recently convinced a Christian music trio to perform her songs almost exclusively, and even persuaded them to concentrate on performing and recording while she wrote songs for them and managed the group. As of this writing they are negotiating a deal with Word Records.

How long will it take to become established?

Without trying to sound flip: as long as it takes to get your first hit. Or to sell your first 5,000 to 10,000 CDs.

How do I price my work?

Many new songwriters incorrectly speak of "selling songs." Selling songs outright has been illegal for years. You can not approach a publisher and sell him all the rights to a song for a fee. He might "sign" the song, giving him the right to promote it. And he might pay advances against future expected royalties, but he can't outright buy a song. (Commercial jingles selling a product are the exception to this rule).

For that reason there's no selling involved with most songs. You write it, sign an agreement with a publisher, and collect your royalties.

If you are offered a single song contract from a publisher, have an entertainment lawyer review it to ensure you're getting a fair deal on the major points. Don't be a jerk though and fight over every point. That's the sign of an amateur.

For more important contracts such as signing an agreement with a major label as a singer-songwriter or a contract involving assignment of publishing rights on a song you've written that is already a hit, more detailed legal wrangling is expected.

Pricing your self-published songs is even easier. Visit major record stores to see what similar work sells for and price your project accordingly unless you believe it has some inherent value that buyers will be willing to pay above average prices for.

How difficult is this nut to crack?

It depends on which facet of the business you pursue. In the 70's and early 80's the state of the freelance songwriting business was dismal. If you weren't able to write hits for major or top independent label acts, there were few other avenues you were likely to make much income from, save perhaps writing songs for commercials. Technology and the Internet have opened up exciting revenue sources for songwriters. Songs are needed for commercial websites, cable TV, movies, and more. Several Internet sites that give new songwriters exposure, and some that actually pay indie songwriters every time their songs are downloaded, have survived the Internet dot com meltdown and appear to have sound business models that will keep them solvent for some time to come. One songwriter is even offering an online service writing songs for client's birthdays, that appears to be quite successful!

That being said, of all the endeavors in this book, songwriting is still the most difficult to break into, especially if you narrow your focus strictly to writing hits for major label artists, as the songwriter mentioned in the next section of the book did. But perseverance can overcome just about anything...

On Perseverance and Co-Writing

A great example of a songwriter persevering and succeeding big is songwriter, Louis Cate. As a publisher (Listen Again Music) I signed a song of his named *Restless Heart* in 1987. I failed to get it cut, so the rights reverted to Lou. In spite of that and other setbacks, he continued writing. His tenacity paid off. In the *1999 Songwriter's Market*, Lou is credited with writing a song called *Heartbreak* for country superstar Trisha Yearwood.

If ten years sounds like too long to wait for success, consider co-writing (writing songs with a partner or multiple partners). If any one of your co-writers succeeds, it will benefit you as well. Some of my co-writers have continued marketing songs for years after I forgot I'd ever been involved in the project. It's a networking tool that creates marketing synergy. Wouldn't you rather have 50 people pushing your songs instead of just you?

Forming Your Own Publishing Company

Should you choose to record and release your own songs (the indie artist path mentioned earlier in the chapter) you'll need to form a music publishing company. In fact, anyone involved in the music business may encounter a situation where having a publishing company would be beneficial, usually when a song is about to receive significant radio airplay.

First, you must name your company, and for that, the rules are the same as they are for any business you might start. Check your state and local ordinances, of course, but few areas have restrictions on sole proprietorships beyond requiring a license should you choose a fictional name (as opposed to using your own last name in the business name).

Step two is to join a PRO (performing rights organization). BMI, ASCAP, and SESAC are the three biggest PROs. They collect royalties from performance venues and distribute them to members.

Some song publishing companies engage principally in copyright administration, some function as song agents, while others are more like management/publishing companies, packaging acts (who perform the publisher's songs) and promoting them. The end game is to either sell the act to a major label or release product directly to the public.

All three PROs mentioned above have offices in Los Angeles, Nashville, and New York. For additional information visit BMI.com, ASCAP.com and SESAC.com.

For Further Study:

The following 6 titles are available from Creative Books:

Songwriter's Market. This is the bible for marketing songs. Don't even think of starting a songwriting career without a recent copy. Detailed listings of over 2,000 places to send your songs. Includes names, addresses, phone numbers, e-mails of major publishers, producers and record companies. How much they pay staff writers is listed. It also gives submission details, lists recent songs they've published or produced and much more. Updated annually. The most recent edition published will be shipped. $24.50.

How to Successfully Market Your Songs and Plan Your Songwriting Career. This is a report, not a book, but it is jammed packed with in-depth, quality information on song marketing that simply doesn't exist anywhere else; It's recommended that you pick up a copy because reading this report can mean the difference between succeeding and failing for 99% of songwriters. plus it's only $15, post paid. ($19 U.S. for Canadian orders). In fact if you can only afford to purchase three products right now, get this report, a copy of *Songwriter's Market* and *The Craft of Lyric Writing*.

The Craft of Lyric Writing by Sheila Davis. Teaches specific techniques and how to employ them. Don't attempt to write a professional lyric without reading this book first. $25.50.

The Craft and Business of Songwriting. by John Braheny. A good choice for getting an in-depth rundown on the entire industry. $23.50.

Music Publishing: A Songwriter's Guide by Randy Poe. How to choose the best royalty agreements. Covers: grand rights, mechanical licenses, various contracts. Copyright protection. Takes the mystery out of the publishing side of songwriting. $20.50.

The Songwriter's Guide to Song & Demo Submission Formats. This book includes dozens of sample query letters that will help get your foot in the door of major publishers. Authoritative instructions for packaging and pitching songs and music. $21.50.

Making and Selling Your Own CD's and Cassettes by Jana Stanfield. Triple platinum singer/songwriter Jana Stanfield shares her experience in this complete guide to having a successful songwriting career without signing a major label deal. $19.50.

Orders for the above 7 titles should be sent to:

Creative Books
P. O. Box 463
Beaver, PA 15009-0463

Check or money order only. Prices include shipping and handling and the most recent edition in print will be shipped. Should a price increase occur, you will be notified (or send extra and the overpayment will be refunded). PA residents must add 6% sales tax. Add $10 for Canadian orders.

If you need demos of your songs produced, Play It Again Demos specializes in that service. For pricing, a free, informative newsletter, customer testimonials, and more, visit: www.forcomm.net/playitagain

The Play It Again sister site, www.billwatson.net focuses on music and writing education. It features beginner and intermediate level articles you may access at no charge. At the time of this writing the three most popular article topics posted at the site were:

Marketing Songs To Publishers
Copyrighting Your Songs
Working With A Demo Service

Another title you might wish to keep handy as you write:

The Modern Songwriter's Rhyming Dictionary by Gene Lees. Cherry Lane Books. ISBN: 0-892524-129-3. Stuck for a fresh rhyme? This book will help you find one.

No Internet access? You can also contact the three largest performing rights organizations by phone:

BMI: Nashville (615) 401-2000
 New York (615) 401-2000
Los Angeles (310) 659-9109

SESAC (headquarters in Nashville, TN)
615-320-0055

ASCAP: 1-800-952-7227

Chapter 13

Should You Be On the Internet?

It seems like all you hear about on the news these days is how the "Internet is the future" or "The Internet is changing the way business is conducted." In 1997 I even heard one supposed "expert" on TV say: "By the year 2000, any business that isn't on the net will be history."

Ridiculous. It's 1999 and there are plenty of thriving businesses that have no connection to the Internet and that's not likely to change in a few months. Maybe even ever.

For some business operators, having a website is truly their path to riches. For others, the Internet is a bust. Many businesses with web sites up, with meta tags (part of a site's HTML programming) in place, and with high placement in search engines (search engines are directories people can look through to find your web page), are seeing zero sales, or close to it.

Many corporate web sites, online magazines, online malls, and companies whose stock is zooming on wall street just because of hype about the net are actually losing money.

The Internet has problems when it comes to transacting business. It's slow, it's frustrating at times, and it's often difficult to find exactly what you're looking for. Even "secure servers" which are supposed to allow you to complete credit card transactions without fear of having your number stolen don't make all potential buyers feel secure after years of hearing "never put personal information on the net."

But isn't the Internet growing at a fantastic rate? "They" say it is. But they always report in terms of "40,000 new people went online last week." What they don't reveal is how many people *disconnected*. Most leave because they are disgusted with the pornography that abounds on online, or because they have children they want to shield from it (and automatic shielding programs don't always eliminate it), or because they have a spouse who became addicted to chat rooms. Some people disconnect because it's too time consuming. Some find it boring. Face it: Internet growth is slowing. The people who aren't online now don't want to be or can't afford it. There will be some additional penetration of the not-currently-online market but the only huge, untapped potential growth areas are overseas, and foreign customers are more difficult for a small business to market to profitably.

Personally, I have little problem with the Internet. I think it's a fantastic business tool. And I've grown with it, having had a website nearly from its inception. At first, I had a much better success ratio converting inquiries into customers using traditional advertising. Over the past two years; however, orders have increased.

Grab your board

Many novice entrepreneurs get caught up in Internet hype, especially those who dislike networking, phone calls and/or face-to-face contact. They figure they'll eliminate all that personal contact stuff by tossing up a web page. Once they're exposed to the "global market," orders will start rolling in.

They invest a lot of time and sometimes significant amounts of money setting up an online site. Sometimes, *rarely*, it actually works. There *are* success stories, like I said. But usually, it just doesn't fly.

If you're considering setting up a stock photography page, or a website promoting your plant growing business or a page to sell your self-published book, by all means, do so. In fact, I encourage it, but I'm against spending thousands of dollars of valuable cash flow on it unless your business is completely dependent on e-commerce. Even then, don't overdo it. Overspending on website development and maintenance is one of the reasons why many "big dot coms who could do no wrong in the 90s" are now defunct. Start small and improve your site as your cash flow increases, that's the surer path to success.

A website can be a great supplement to your business, but that's all it may ever be. Think of it as an excellent, inexpensive marketing tool rather than as a way to actually close sales. If nothing else, it will improve your image. A site will probably produce at least some sales, too. And once again, properly designed, it shouldn't require much maintenance.

If it does bring in huge profits, great, but don't get your hopes up. The wild card in this whole deck is: we can't see what the future holds. Perhaps the Internet *will* achieve it's promise. If so, it can't hurt to be positioned where you can catch the very first wave to the beach of plenty.

But you said the Internet is a fantastic business tool

It is:

- As a writer, I've used e-mail to submit assigned manuscripts and to send supplements to previously submitted material, easily meeting tight deadlines that would have been impossible by regular mail.

- For my nursery, I've found sources of seeds, seedlings, and full-size stock at prices far below what I was previously paying.

- My recording studio has *occasionally* obtained jobs through from the studio's web site.

- As a songwriter, I've found co-writers online.

- My landscape business now has free, 24-hour-a-day access to radar.

- I've saved money on phone calls and postage many times by using e-mail when responding to customer requests.

- It's great for things like researching equipment purchases, checking facts with experts on various subjects, and comparing financing.

- Online forums and e-mail newsletters keep me up-to-date in the fields I'm currently engaged in such as publishing, writing, recording, etc.

- My businesses have attained new customers in England, Kenya, Ireland, Germany, the West Indies, and more because of the web.

And that's just a sample of the many benefits I derive from being online.

So should I go online or not?

The computer is the most expensive component of getting connected and if you tell a computer salesmen you're starting a business soon, he'll try to convince you that you "must" have a computer and must be online to run a business. If you're starting up a manufacturing concern with a million dollar loan and have ten employees starting the first day, I'd have to agree. To start any of the businesses in *this* book, a computer or Internet connection is not absolutely necessary with three possible exceptions: writing, self-publishing, and developing a music career as an independent artist. The advantages to marketing online for those endeavors are quite clear. If you're writing songs and releasing CDs, online sites such as MP3.com, that pay unsigned songwriters for CD sales and downloads, can provide essential cash flow. And anything involving publishing or writing is best done on a computer. Keeping books, tracking inventory, and figuring taxes can be done by hand at first (if necessary) in any of the businesses in this book.

If you already have a computer, by all means, use it. If you can afford one easily and still have enough money for your other start-up costs, purchase one. But use it and/or your online connection wisely. They can be time savers or time wasters; they can be profit makers or profit takers. Disks, paper, software programs, and ink for your printer will eat up valuable cash, while learning to use the computer and learning to navigate the Internet eats up (not saves) time you need to learn your business.

If money is tight, you don't have a computer yet, and don't know how to build a webpage yourself, build your business off-line, then buy a computer and go online when you can afford it. The Internet may or may not work well for you but the computer itself will be an *essential* tool when your business expands.

Chapter 14

Planning Your Career Path

To succeed at any of the businesses in this book, it is absolutely imperative that you understand exactly what you're getting into and formulate a realistic plan for your career. Not necessarily a formal business plan, though it could be. At minimum you need to commit to paper an outline of what you expect from your business, what you hope to achieve in it, and a concrete list of efforts you must put into the business to achieve your goals.

As a rule, "creativity-required" businesses or careers take longer to achieve success in than say, opening a pizza shop. To some "wanna-be's" talking in terms of years turns them off. If you aren't willing to commit to a long-term plan, then you should find some other line of work.

It's easy to understand why those uninitiated to the realities of business expect things to be easier than they are. Believing creativity is some unique trait, they reason that few people are blessed with talent; therefore, if they enter a certain field, within a short time they'll almost automatically rise to the top. (Please re-read chapter two if you're still thinking that). When that doesn't happen, and it almost never does, they become disillusioned, realize it's harder than they thought, then 99% quit, leaving the 1% who stick it out to reap the rewards. Even when the realities are clearly explained, most new entrepreneurs figure they'll be the exception to the rule. Somehow they have extra talent that "the powers that be" in that field will notice and they'll be on their way, if not to the top, at least halfway up the ladder.

Horsecrap.

It's not ridiculous to expect to take years to make it in certain professions. How many years does it take to become a C.P.A.? A Doctor? A Lawyer? If you reach the top in most of the careers in this book, you'll be paid more than many doctors and lawyers so why should it take you any less time to master your craft? Especially when you're entering a career that's more glamorous and consequently more competitive than being a doctor or lawyer. Why wouldn't you have to invest money and time to learn just as a doctor, C.P.A. or lawyer does?

Re-read the chapter on the field you intend to enter. As you read, begin diagramming a career path for yourself based on the information provided. If it's an enterprise where you're advised to expect difficulties, rejections, long "break-in" times, and the like, then set your mind right now: that's the way it's going to be. Should it take less time then consider yourself extremely lucky.

As an example, here's a realistic sample career path for someone wishing to enter the writing field:

Goal # 1: Have four magazine articles accepted for publication in the first eight months. (Note: That doesn't seem very ambitious but it is. It takes time to order sample magazines, subscriptions, and writer's guides and receive them. It takes time to mold your raw writing talent into an effective query letter form. It then takes even longer to submit queries to enough magazines to find one you "match" with).

Means to achieve that goal: Learn to write effective query letters. Order the appropriate books to learn everything possible to avoid wasting months or years of time and totally wasting essential start-up funds solving problems that can be solved in a few minutes of reading.

Possible difficulties or delays: 1. Time will be wasted weeding out publications that are unsuitable for one reason or another. 2. It will likely take at least 20 letters before an effective query writing style starts to develop. 3. Even when a good query is targeted effectively it may take two or three months for the editor to respond. 4. Some assignments may be "blown" due to a lack of experience when writing the actual manuscript. 5. It may be necessary to write "on spec" or free at first to get a foot in the door.

Main "career-stopper" to avoid- allowing rejections to dampen enthusiasm. Solution: Send a minimum of 100 queries regardless of the results of the early submissions, expecting all 100 to be rejected. Let any acceptances be pleasant surprises, then get back to work.

Goal #2: In the next 16 month period have 32 articles published.

This accelerated pace assumes that effective query and manuscript writing has been mastered and several "ins" have been made with editors, cutting wasted queries.

Goal #3: Once 100 articles have been published in national magazines, begin work on a book.

Means to achieve goal: 1. Order *How to Write A Book Proposal* and some type of how-to on book writing. 2. Start researching and writing the book, then query until 50 proposals have been sent.

Possible difficulties- 1. Finding a publisher. Solution: pre-qualify possible publishers in Writer's Market. If after 50 proposals are rejected or ignored, self-publish with a thorough marketing plan.

Goal #4: Continually increase income and enter more prestigious markets with the aim of making writing a sole source of income within five years of start-up.

Your career plan can be far more detailed if you wish and can include income goals at specific points. The only real requirement is that you must realistically think through each key stepping stone in your career, anticipate potential difficulties and solutions to them and set realistic expectations.

* * *

As you read this book you may find yourself pulled in more than one direction. You may consider yourself a musician for example, but find yourself attracted to the landscaping field because the money seems better or steadier. Or perhaps you wanted to be a wildlife photographer but now that you see how long it can take and why, self-publishing is looking more realistic.

One thing that might help you sort out this duality is to ask yourself: "Am I in love with photographing wildlife, or in love with the *idea* of being a wildlife photographer." If the answer is that you're in love with the idea, there's a chance you might not even enjoy the daily grind of wildlife photography.

Have you considered what that daily grind will entail? Taking a photo, singing a song, or whatever is fun, no one would argue that. But taking pictures day after day in all types of weather conditions, or singing songs night after night regardless of whether you have a cold or don't feel like facing an audience, might not be such a blast.

And there may be other drawbacks- if, for example, you become a "big-time" musician you might spend a lot of time riding buses city to city.

Every job in this world has less-than-glamorous aspects. Duane Allman once said he'd rather be playing his guitar and starve than be rich doing anything else. If you are truly a musician then the joys of playing the music will make up for any disadvantages that career path may hold. And there may be nothing else you *could* do and be happy. Ditto any other career in this book.

However if you are merely in love with the idea of being known as a songwriter or whatever, then you may find that you could just as easily switch to some other creative endeavor and do quite well at it, reasoning that since you must work at something. you'd rather do something interesting and creative with your life than work a more mundane job.

* * *

If you wish to pursue a multi-faceted career keep in mind that it's extra-difficult to pull off because of the inherent inefficiencies that come with a lack of focus. You can do it though if you..

1. Master one thing at a time. Read everything you can about your chosen activity. You must become an expert and establish a profitable "flagship" business before you dilute your efforts by branching out.

2. Strip that business down to only the most profitable jobs or customers and the most essential, high-quality equipment. The best way to do that? Start raising your prices on your least profitable activities or customers. This will raise profits while cutting back on your workload. Sell equipment that isn't super-dependable and in constant use.

3. Focus on presenting an image of quality to the customer. This is part of how you'll justify your higher prices. The other part? You're now an expert. Experts are worth more.

4. Raise the price you charge to near the top end of the scale. Be careful. You don't want to wreck your business but you do need to focus only on the highly profitable activities or jobs.

5. Now you have the time and money to tackle an additional business. Start the whole process over.

How Long Should You Try Before Giving Up?

In "creativity-required" businesses, a moderately-talented person with a will to "stick things out" will outdistance a super-talented person who lacks perseverance every time. But at what point does perseverance turn into idiocy? At what point should you say enough's enough?

First, you must give your career a fighting chance. If a career requires five years to get established and you give up after two years, then you're quitting prematurely. This book states certain time frames to accomplish something only as a very general guideline for an average (but talented) person under average circumstances. Your schedule may be a little slower than average for many reasons, some of which may be totally beyond your control.

Now if you've been plugging away much beyond double the time frame you expected to reach a certain point in your career and you truly believe you've given the effort required, (learned enough to consider yourself an expert on the subject, invested as much money as necessary, and put forth ample amounts of time and energy) then it's time to re-assess the situation. Consider trying an easier business, or at least realize that you might be mistaken about your talent. If you choose to continue on, know that you may never get further in this endeavor than the hobby level.

* * *

The author's view: Don't fall victim to the "Never give up and you'll make it" advice that flourishes in certain books, magazines and TV shows. Inevitably that counsel comes from someone who "made it" after continuing to try for many years beyond what a reasonable person would have. They are giving that advice because that's what worked for them. In their tiny frame of reference it seems to be true.

Because they are famous they get interviewed. No one interviews the guy who heard that advice, believed it, and is now living in a cardboard box, having squandered most of his life and all his money in a failed attempt to become a rock star.

I believe a person should set reasonable limits on how long they'll pursue something unsuccessfully. If you haven't become a rock star by age 35, regardless of when you started, chances are you never will when you consider most record companies that deal in rock only sign new artists who are teens and early twenty-somethings. None of the businesses in this book have any real age limits per se, but it's a good idea to have an exit plan as part of your career path. Besides, cardboard boxes look like they'd be difficult to heat in the winter without catching them on fire.

There's another very real threat to your longevity in business. I call it the "success then quit" syndrome. When a person struggles a long time, then finally reaches a minor career goal, it can cause a sense of accomplishment out of proportion to the achievement followed by a loss of enthusiasm for the business. I've experienced it several times: when I had my first song accepted by a publisher, when I had my first article accepted by a major magazine, when I completed installing my first huge landscape project, and when my band opened for a national act for the first time. Within a short time of each of those events I had virtually quit each business. I say virtually because while I quit one of those activities outright, in the other cases my body was still in the business but my mind wasn't into it at all.

What happens? My belief is: often these events come when you least expect it, just when you've started thinking nothing is going to happen. Suddenly this exciting event occurs. Simultaneously, you experience excitement and feel you've reached a milestone in your career. The event passes, the excitement fades, then you have to face going back to the drudgery of routine to try to make it happen again. Soon your subconscious starts convincing you that "you've made it now", that "there's nothing more you need to prove." If you believe those lies, you'll quit at the pinnacle of your career.

You can be so focused on a short-term goal that takes a few years to achieve that it can start to seem like it's the end goal. You may forget there are other goals beyond it. Avoid this trap by concentrating more on long-term goals rather than short-term. And have a plan to re-focus your energies on the next step as each goal is met.

Chapter 15

The Future of These Creativity-Required Businesses

During the past twenty five years, many "creativity-required" activities have gone through a great deal of upheaval just as most other businesses have. Advancing technology and economic realignments have opened new opportunities while closing off others. In the businesses covered in this book, most of the changes have improved working conditions without much affecting the core product or service, but some individual jobs have been eliminated altogether. In general: the future looks bright for all these activities but an in-depth look at changes that have occurred in the past few years and what to expect is in order:

Self Publishing: Computers have turned this business upside down. From designing covers and sales materials, to typesetting, to billing customers, it can all be done on an IBM compatible or Mac now. More work can now be completed in-house by the self-publisher, often (not always) saving both time and money.

In the next few years look for faster computers and software with more intense focus, such as easier-to-use newsletter software. The self-publishing field will grow tremendously and there will be a wealth of business start-ups that cater to the outsourcing needs of the self-publisher. Already there are more short-run (as few as one hundred books) and on-demand (printing each copy as it's needed) book printers who work directly with the disks a self-publisher creates.

This is the information age. As long as you can give people information they want or need, this business appears to be solid for many years to come.

Photography: Digital technology is establishing itself as the future of photography. The 35mm camera is still the choice of most professionals but that will likely change. Pros are already embracing computer programs that enhance analog images after the fact, and in October of 2000, Eastman Kodak announced they had successfully created digital sensors that could furnish twice the resolution of 35mm.

Expect continued improvement in film and equipment (to try to keep pace with digital) and increasingly higher standards for all professional photographers to meet.

If you're entering the wedding photography field, consider offering videotaping services along with still photography.

Magazine photography depends a great deal on the health of the industry it feeds. Right now, with some 30,000 titles, print magazines appear to be going strong, but as postage, paper and printing costs rise there will be a continual weeding out of magazines in publication over the next ten years.

Landscaping: The biggest changes have been in equipment and the computer design of landscapes. Gone are the huge dinosaur earth-moving machines, replaced by smaller, faster, more efficient skid-steer loaders with attachments like plant augers, tree carriers and the like. Now even smaller, more specialized equipment such as mini-loaders and machines designed solely for bed work are on the market and increasing in popularity.

This is a huge-money field, consequently a lot of equipment manufacturing firms spend large amounts of time and money on R&D so expect significant equipment changes with an emphasis on ease-of-use and elimination of expensive labor. Owners will see increased profitability with fewer workers. Of course, that's not real good news if you happen to be one of the workers who is no longer needed.

Overall this field looks very strong for many years into the future.

Recording: Technology has dramatically changed this industry. Synthesizers, digital recorders, and drum machines have made producing commercial product less labor intensive, while improved home recording equipment has reduced business for mid-grade studios. High-end studios have actually seen increases in work as more musicians get involved in home recording. When it's time for a "big" project the musicians choose the highest quality studio available rather than a studio that can't deliver much better quality than what they have at home.

Mid-grade multi-purpose studios will probably decline in profitability over the next ten years while specialized project studios and high-end facilities will hold their own or witness an increase in work available.

Plant Growing: The means to grow plants and the techniques used to grow them have improved steadily in the last couple of decades, a trend that will continue. Look for improvements in fertilizers, soilless mixes and more products to make growing more efficient. For example: growers knew for years that copper on the inside of pots stopped root growth upon contact but only recently has science produced a medium that suspends copper in a solution that can be applied to pots and won't break down when watered. Sold under various brand names, it's changing the way ornamentals are grown.

Studies are being conducted on various plants that will result in improved growing techniques. The thrust of these studies will be on decreasing production time while improving quality.

Plant sales are expected to remain strong for the foreseeable future.

Magazine Article and Book Writing: The only significant change in this field in the past few years is a huge one: word processing, which has made writing a far easier, more pleasant task. The basic techniques of writing have changed very little.

Right now, the book industry has shown slightly increased sales in spite of competition from other entertainment media such as TV and movies. Many writers report having an easier time getting book proposals accepted and receiving higher advances than ever before.

The magazine industry is very strong which bodes well for writers. The wild card in this field is the Internet. Right now Internet E-zines are not profitable as a group as people seem to prefer reading printed copy rather than information on a computer screen. Should people's tastes change or technology develops electronic publications that people will accept, the publishing industry could change rapidly. For the writer though, it would likely mean simply sending off your copy to an e-zine or electronic book editor instead of a print publisher. The person who can write clearly and provide needed information will always be in demand.

Performing Live Music: There is still a great deal of work available for musicians but intoxicated-driver laws (doesn't that sound better than drunk driving laws?) and disc jockeys have seriously reduced the live music work available in bars and clubs. Technology such as Midi has reduced the need for keyboard players while drum machines and synthesizers (capable of imitating practically any sound) have virtually eliminated the need for many instruments. Pro singers, drummers, guitarists, keyboardists, and bassists can still find enough live work to make a living. Other instruments like sax, fiddle, banjo, squeeze boxes (popular in Zydeco), and quite a few other instruments, while not used in every type of music, are hired by certain bands as well.

Technology can only continue on the path it's started. Look for improvements in the ease of utilizing computer-generated music in bands which will lead to smaller units- three-piece groups who sound like 6 for example. The musicians who focus on providing entertainment value, rather than just being technically proficient on their instrument, have the most promising futures. There will always be work for great entertainers.

Also look for the development of audience machines. Since musicians can so easily be replaced by technology and musicians actually do something, aren't audiences even more useless? All they do is sit there, clap periodically, and use the bathroom every so often. Wouldn't it be easy to make a machine that can sit there and clap? It wouldn't even need to use the bathroom. Plus out-of-work musician's could buy them to remember what playing live actually felt like.

Teaching: Online sites have emerged that offer free lessons in various disciplines, but children and a substantial portion of adults don't learn any better from these sites than they do from self-help books. New techniques come and go, but this business is still about the person-to-person direct exchange of knowlege.

Expect teaching work to remain steady and even increase, especially for those who can adapt their teaching to the Internet.

Songwriting: The music industry is big, rivaling the landscape industry in total dollar revenue- about 14 billion a year- but in the music industry the money is mostly concentrated in the hands of just a few companies and artists, rather than spread among many companies. The landscape industry provides full-time jobs for people in practically every community in the U.S. and the music/songwriting industry could do the same if the airplay system were different. Instead, increasingly restricted radio playlists and large numbers of stations being automatically programmed by one firm have been reducing the need for new songwriters for years. And the situation is expected to continue to decline or at best hold steady over the next several years. Still, a reading of American Songwriter proves that staff writers are hired by publishers almost daily and new writers do hit the charts every year.

The brightest spot for new songwriters, and songwriters who write material that isn't suited well to the major label airplay system, is the Internet. It is certainly changing the way music is distributed and purchased in this country, allowing small record companies and far more songwriters to share in a piece of the music industry pie. Expect increasing resistance to that idea from major labels who don't like the idea of receiving a smaller cut of the proceeds. But the smart money is betting that they will find it's tough to put a genie back once it's out of the bottle.

The task of songwriting itself has not been greatly influenced by technology and probably won't be. The exceptions to that statement are things like trance and techno pop in which recorded samples and loops from other songs become part of the new song. Of course, making song *demos* has been affected by the same technological advances that has affected all music production. Cheaper, better, recording equipment; synthesizers; harmonizers; and midi, allow for better sound at less cost. Even if your demos are done by a service, you still benefit from technology when you receive a $350 demo that sounds better than one you'd have spent $1,000 on fifteen years ago.

The prospects for a career in songwriting are more promising now than in recent years, especially for an artist building an independent career. For the person who can create hit material and market it successfully, the future is quite bright indeed.

* * *

It's Time To Ease On Down The Road

This seems like a pretty good spot to wrap things up. I'm sure I've provided more information about these 9 creativity-required businesses than you needed to know but I'd rather provide too much information than too little.

If your dream is to make a living in one of these enterprises I guarantee you that somewhere in these pages is the right one for you and I pray that you've found it. For your sake, because I found mine a long time ago and know what it's like to really enjoy making a living doing something you love. In my case it's doing a lot of things I love.

Every time I see an article of mine published in a magazine, or plants from my nursery complete a customer's landscape or I listen to a demo I produced for a client, that I know completely captures the feel the writer was trying to convey, I feel a little twinge of pride and experience a tremendous sense of accomplishment. It's a feeling that you can only know by creating something, risk putting it out there for the world to examine, and have it accepted.

Of course the checks you get paid are kinda nice too.

I do hope you've enjoyed the book (my first, by the way) and that you've learned at least one thing you didn't know when we started this journey together. Before we part ways I'd like to leave you with this:

Set your course in this life and follow it with the determination of a bird winging its way to some distant home.

When the winds are against you, when you feel like giving up, persevere my friend, as any creature who has ever accomplished anything worthwhile in this world has done.

Like that resolute little bird you must learn to put your thoughts not on the difficulties of the moment, but fix them firmly on the rewards that await you when you succeed. Do this, and I guarantee you that someday you will reach your destination. And in that moment you will rejoice for the rest of your days.

A list of selected titles available from Creative Books:

Writer's Market- Detailed listings of magazine publishers, book publishers, and other markets for writers. (Updated annually. The latest edition will be shipped.) $29.50

Songwriter's Market. Detailed listings of over 2,000 places to send your songs. Updated annually. The most recent edition published will be shipped. $24.50

Handbook of Magazine Article Writing- A complete guide to the subject. $17.50

Photographer's Market. (annual-the most recent edition will be sent) Detailed listings of 2,000 places to sell your photographs. $25.50

The Craft of Lyric Writing by Sheila Davis. Specific techniques and how to employ them. $25.50

The Complete Guide to Self-Publishing by Tom & Marylin Ross. Advice on all aspects of book publishing and marketing from production to publicity. $21.50

Hot Tips For The Home Recording Studio. by Hank Linderman. A wealth of home recording advice for musicians and beginning producers. $21.50

How to Write Attention-Grabbing Query Letters by John Wood. $19.50

How to Write a Book Proposal. A guide to submitting your manuscript for publication. $17.50

9 Creativity Required Businesses You Can Start From Home by Bill Watson. *$23.95*

Writing Articles About the World Around You by Marcia Yudkin. $19.50

Grammatically Correct by Anne Stilman. How to write concisely and clearly. $21.50

The Musician's Guide to Making and Selling Your Own CD's and Cassettes. $20.50

The Craft and Business of Songwriting. by John Braheny. $23.50

Music Publishing: A Songwriter's Guide. by Randy Poe. The publishing side of songwriting. $20.50

The Songwriter's Guide to Song & Demo Submission Formats. $21.50

The Professional Photographer's Guide to Shooting and Selling Nature and Wildlife Photos. Just what the title says it is. $26.50

Sell & Re-sell your photos. The bible on marketing photos. Filled with example photos, helpful charts, tables, and sidebars. $18.50

The Photographer's Market Guide to Photo Submissions and Portfolio Formats. Detailed, visual examples guide you through the photo submission and selling maze to maximize income from your images. $20.50

Making Money Writing Newsletters by Elaine Floyd. How to set up and run a newsletter production service. Includes 39 forms you can copy and use. $31.50

Jump Start Your Book Sales- A Money-Making Guide for Authors and Publishers. Includes dozens of real-life success stories. *$21.50*

Afterword

The reason this book was written, was to make a point: to achieve success in an endeavor that's based on the creative output of the person who starts it does not require talent beyond the mediocre- *if* the person is good at marketing.

True, there are a few people who are blessed with talent so unique or so great that they are practically destined to "make it." For those of us who aren't, my experience is that plunking on your guitar ten hours a day (or whatever your particular talent is) will eventually make you an excellent guitarist. But not a world-class guitarist. Now it's certainly a great accomplishment to be an excellent guitarist, the problem is- excellent guitarists, writers or whatever, are a dime a dozen.

If I didn't make my point strong enough at the beginning of the book, then let me make it at the end: If you want to start a business or develop a career based on your talent and succeed, then allocate less time to developing your talent and more to marketing it. Follow that advice faithfully and the things you dream about tonight will be your daily life tomorrow....

Just try not to have any nightmares!

INDEX

Need another copy?

9 Creativity-Required Businesses You Can Start From Home

And How to Make Them Profitable Careers

— —

Yes, send me _____ copies of *9 Creativity-Required Businesses You Can Start From Home*. I have enclosed $23.95 which includes shipping for each copy. Discounts are available for orders of 10 copies or more. Allow 2-4 weeks for delivery. Canadian orders are $10 extra. PA residents add $1.44 sales tax.

Ship to:

Name:_____

Address: _____

_____

Zip: _____

Send your order to:

Creative Books
P.O. Box 463
Beaver, PA 15009-0463

Special prices on large quantities available upon request.